e.explore

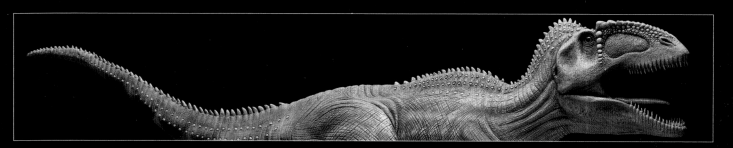

Dinosaur

LONDON, NEW YORK, MELBOURNE,
MUNICH and DELHI

Authors Dougal Dixon, John Malam

Senior Editor Margaret Hynes
Project Editors Fran Baines, Frank Ritter, Miranda Smith

Weblink Editors Clare Lister, Mariza O'Keeffe, Phil Hunt, John Bennett

Managing Editor Camilla Hallinan

Digital Development Manager Fergus Day
Production Erica Rosen
DTP Co-ordinator Toby Beedell
DTP Designers Gavin Brabant, Pete Quinlan

Category Publisher Sue Grabham

Consultant Professor Michael Benton

Senior Designers Neville Graham, Smiljka Surla, Owen Peyton Jones, Yumiko Tahata
Project Designers Janice English, Nick Harris, Rebecca Painter
Illustrators Mark Longworth, Peter Winfield
Cartography Robert Stokes

Managing Art Editor Sophia M Tampakopoulos Turner

Picture Researchers Veneta Bullen, Julia Harris-Voss, Alison Floyd
Picture Librarians Sarah Mills, Karl Strange, Kate Ledwith

Jacket Neal Cobourne

Art Director Simon Webb

First published in Great Britain in 2004
by Dorling Kindersley Limited, 80 Strand, London WC2R 0RL

Penguin Group

A CIP catalogue for this book is available from the British Library.

ISBN-10: 1-4053-1544-X
ISBN-13: 978-1-40531-544-9

Colour reproduction by Colourscan, Singapore
Printed in China by Toppan Printing Co. (Shenzen) Ltd.

Discover more at
www.dk.com

e.explore

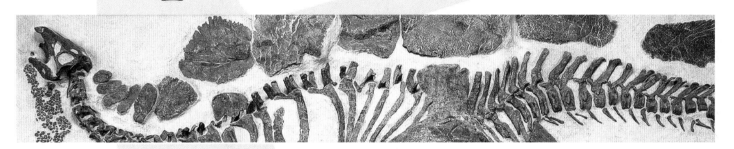

Dinosaur

Written by **Dougal Dixon**
and John Malam

Google

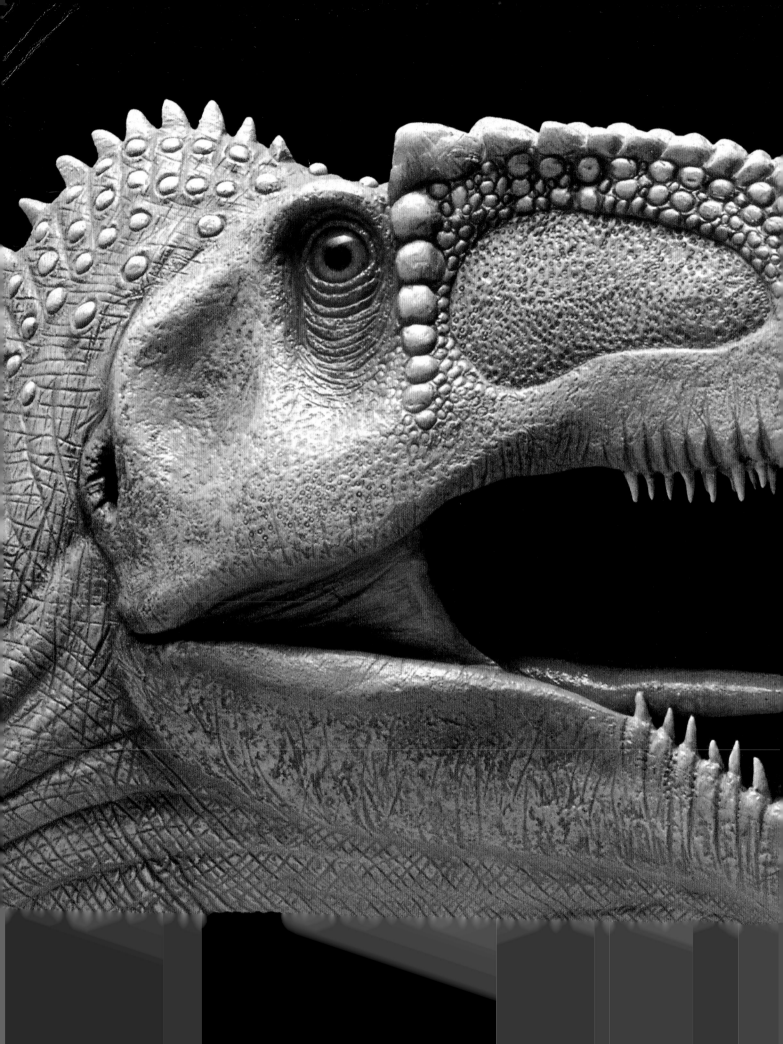

CONTENTS

How to use the e.explore website

e.explore Dinosaur has its own website, created by DK and Google™.
When you look up a subject in the book, the article gives you key facts
and displays a keyword that links you to extra information online.
Just follow these easy steps.

http://www.dinosaur.dke-explore.com

1 Enter this website address...

Address : @ http://www.dinosaur.dke-explore.com

2 Find the keyword in the book...

fossils

3 Enter the keyword...

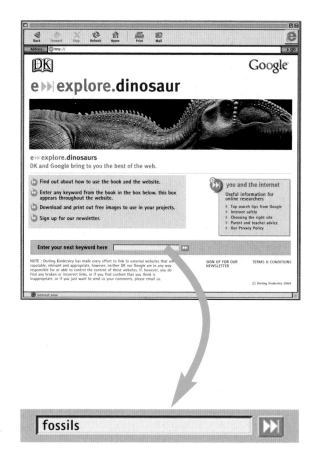

fossils

You can only use the keywords from the book to search
on our website for the specially selected DK/Google links.

Be safe while you are online:

- Always get permission from an adult before connecting to the internet.

- Never give out personal information about yourself.

- Never arrange to meet someone you have talked to online.

- If a site asks you to log in with your name or email address, ask permission from an adult first.

- Do not reply to emails from strangers – tell an adult.

Parents: Dorling Kindersley actively and regularly reviews and updates the links. However, content may change. Dorling Kindersley is not responsible for any site but its own. We recommend that children are supervised while online, that they do not use Chat Rooms, and that filtering software is used to block unsuitable material.

Click on your chosen link...

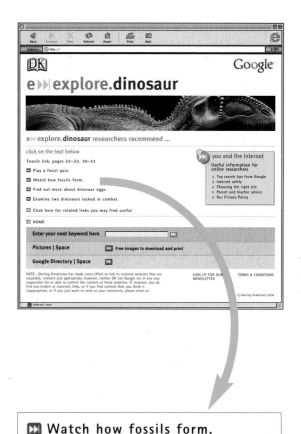

Download fantastic pictures...

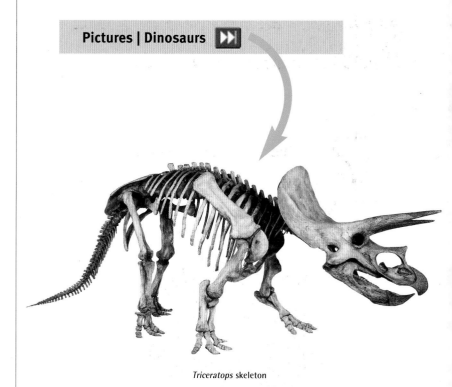

Triceratops skeleton

▶▶ **Watch how fossils form.**

Links include animations, videos, sound buttons, virtual tours, interactive quizzes, databases, timelines, and realtime reports.

The pictures are free of charge, but can be used for personal non-commercial use only.

Go back to the book for your next subject...

WHAT IS A DINOSAUR?

In the middle of the 19th century, the first fossil skeletons of some extraordinary creatures were unearthed. These skeletons are of the dinosaurs – prehistoric reptiles that have captured the imaginations of people ever since. Dinosaurs, which means "terrible lizards", ruled the world for more than 160 million years before they died out 65 million years ago. Everything we know about them has come from the examination of skeletons, or bits of skeletons, found by palaeontologists, the dinosaur-hunters of the modern world, and by other scientists.

▼ GIGANOTOSAURUS
To find out more about the remains that are found, scientists reconstruct dinosaurs, sometimes from only a few fragments of fossilized bone or a skull. The fossils of this *Giganotosaurus* have told scientists a great deal about how this creature lived. The way that the hips and legs are put together shows that it was able to run after prey. The clawed feet and rows of teeth are evidence that once *Giganotosaurus* had caught the prey, the carnivore was equipped to tear it apart.

Head of femur fits into hip socket

Hip bone

Femur (thigh bone)

Tibia (shin bone)

HYPSILOPHODON
ORNITHISCHIAN
("BIRD-HIPPED")

GALLIMIMUS
SAURISCHIAN
("LIZARD-HIPPED")

TYRANNOSAURUS
HIND LIMBS

Hips and legs allowed dinosaur to move feet easily forwards and backwards

▲ LEG BONES
Dinosaurs were archosaurs – a group of reptiles that contained crocodiles, alligators, and flying pterosaurs. However, the legs of most reptiles stick out at the side and the body is slung beneath. Those of a dinosaur are more like those of a mammal. They are vertical, supporting the weight of the body above them. There is a ball-shaped plug at the head of the thigh bone (femur) that protrudes sideways. This fits into a socket in the side of the hip bones. A shelf of bone above the socket prevents the leg from popping out.

▲ HIP BONES
Dinosaurs are divided into two separate groups based on the structure of their hip bones. The groups are called the "saurischians" and the "ornithischians". The saurischians had hip bones like a modern lizard – the three hip bones radiating away from the socket that held the leg, and the pubis bone pointing down and forwards. The ornithischians had hip bones like a modern bird – the pubis sweeping back along the ischium, while a pair of extensions to the pubis reached forward.

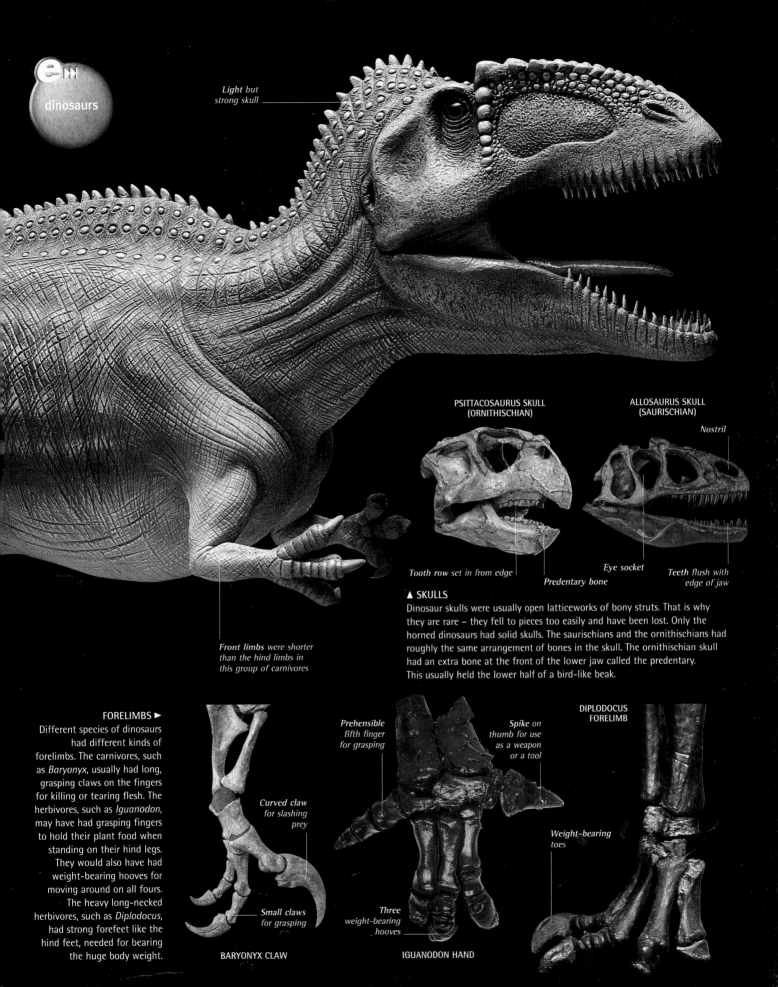

dinosaurs

Light but
strong skull

PSITTACOSAURUS SKULL
(ORNITHISCHIAN)

ALLOSAURUS SKULL
(SAURISCHIAN)

Nostril

Tooth row set in from edge

Predentary bone

Eye socket

Teeth flush with
edge of jaw

▲ SKULLS

Dinosaur skulls were usually open latticeworks of bony struts. That is why
they are rare – they fell to pieces too easily and have been lost. Only the
horned dinosaurs had solid skulls. The saurischians and the ornithischians had
roughly the same arrangement of bones in the skull. The ornithischian skull
had an extra bone at the front of the lower jaw called the predentary.
This usually held the lower half of a bird-like beak.

Front limbs were shorter
than the hind limbs in
this group of carnivores

FORELIMBS ►

Different species of dinosaurs
had different kinds of
forelimbs. The carnivores, such
as *Baryonyx*, usually had long,
grasping claws on the fingers
for killing or tearing flesh. The
herbivores, such as *Iguanodon*,
may have had grasping fingers
to hold their plant food when
standing on their hind legs.
They would also have had
weight-bearing hooves for
moving around on all fours.
The heavy long-necked
herbivores, such as *Diplodocus*,
had strong forefeet like the
hind feet, needed for bearing
the huge body weight.

Curved claw
for slashing
prey

Small claws
for grasping

BARYONYX CLAW

Prehensible
fifth finger
for grasping

Spike on
thumb for use
as a weapon
or a tool

Three
weight-bearing
hooves

IGUANODON HAND

DIPLODOCUS
FORELIMB

Weight-bearing
toes

THE BIRD CONNECTION

There are dinosaurs flying in our skies today – despite more than a century of arguments, most scientists now believe that small meat-eating dinosaurs evolved into birds. The development of feathers turned dinosaurs that could run or climb into birds that could fly. The earliest true bird is *Archaeopteryx*, which lived during the late Jurassic in the area known today as southern Germany. A small hunting dinosaur called *Compsognathus* also lived in that area at that time. *Archaeopteryx* looked like a cross between a reptile and a bird, and it had strong legs and feathers that it would have used to fly. *Compsognathus* was bird-like, with long back legs and hollow bones.

SIMILARITIES BETWEEN COMPSOGNATHUS AND ARCHAEOPTERYX

1 Bony tail core

2 Ankle joint

3 Long legs

4 Short body

5 Enlarged breast bone

6 Teeth in long, slim jaws

7 Slim, flexible neck

8 Long, clawed fingers

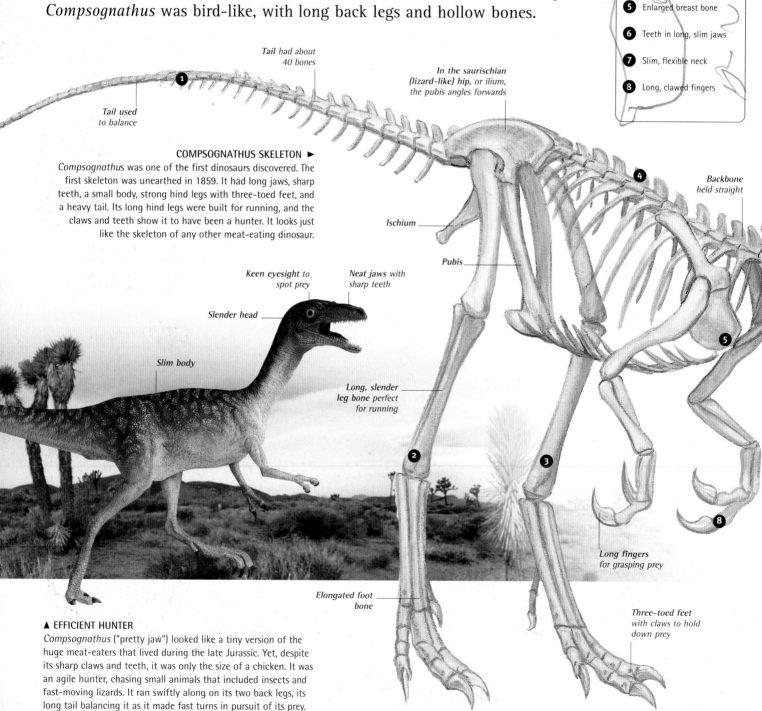

Tail had about 40 bones

In the saurischian (lizard-like) hip, or ilium, the pubis angles forwards

Tail used to balance

COMPSOGNATHUS SKELETON ▶
Compsognathus was one of the first dinosaurs discovered. The first skeleton was unearthed in 1859. It had long jaws, sharp teeth, a small body, strong hind legs with three-toed feet, and a heavy tail. Its long hind legs were built for running, and the claws and teeth show it to have been a hunter. It looks just like the skeleton of any other meat-eating dinosaur.

Backbone held straight

Ischium

Pubis

Keen eyesight to spot prey

Neat jaws with sharp teeth

Slender head

Slim body

Long, slender leg bone perfect for running

Long fingers for grasping prey

Elongated foot bone

Three-toed feet with claws to hold down prey

▲ **EFFICIENT HUNTER**
Compsognathus ("pretty jaw") looked like a tiny version of the huge meat-eaters that lived during the late Jurassic. Yet, despite its sharp claws and teeth, it was only the size of a chicken. It was an agile hunter, chasing small animals that included insects and fast-moving lizards. It ran swiftly along on its two back legs, its long tail balancing it as it made fast turns in pursuit of its prey.

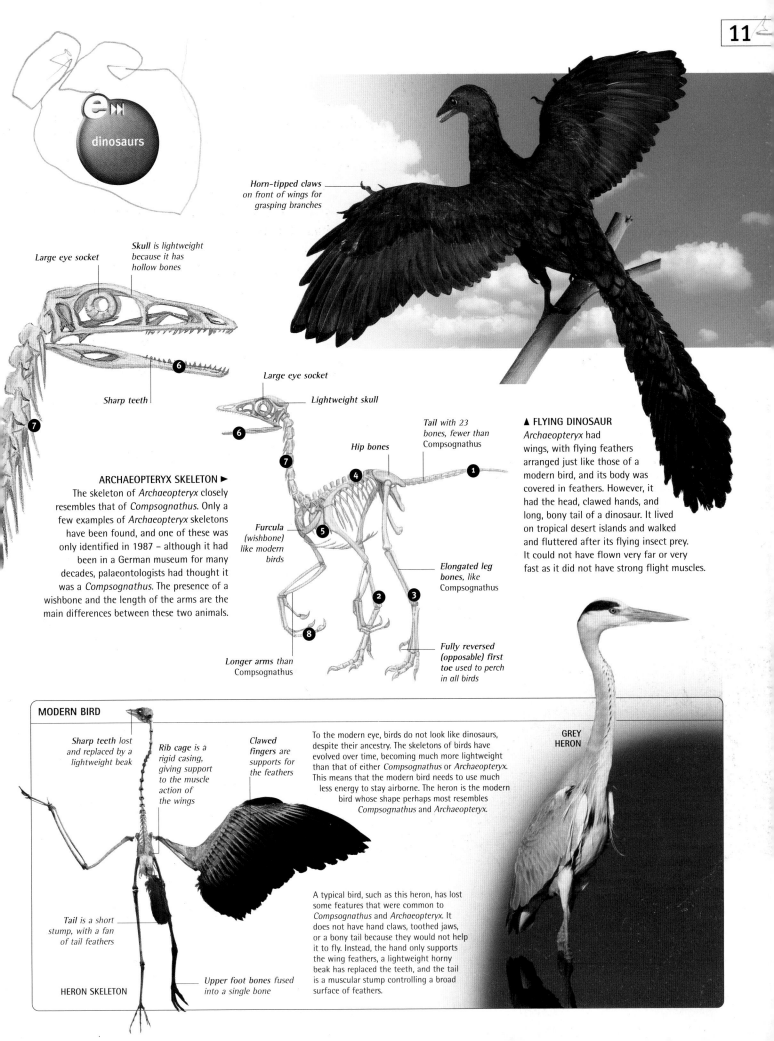

dinosaurs

Horn-tipped claws on front of wings for grasping branches

Large eye socket

Skull is lightweight because it has hollow bones

Sharp teeth

ARCHAEOPTERYX SKELETON ▶

The skeleton of *Archaeopteryx* closely resembles that of *Compsognathus*. Only a few examples of *Archaeopteryx* skeletons have been found, and one of these was only identified in 1987 – although it had been in a German museum for many decades, palaeontologists had thought it was a *Compsognathus*. The presence of a wishbone and the length of the arms are the main differences between these two animals.

Large eye socket

Lightweight skull

Hip bones

Tail with 23 bones, fewer than Compsognathus

Furcula (wishbone) like modern birds

Elongated leg bones, like Compsognathus

Longer arms than Compsognathus

Fully reversed (opposable) first toe used to perch in all birds

▲ FLYING DINOSAUR

Archaeopteryx had wings, with flying feathers arranged just like those of a modern bird, and its body was covered in feathers. However, it had the head, clawed hands, and long, bony tail of a dinosaur. It lived on tropical desert islands and walked and fluttered after its flying insect prey. It could not have flown very far or very fast as it did not have strong flight muscles.

GREY HERON

MODERN BIRD

Sharp teeth lost and replaced by a lightweight beak

Rib cage is a rigid casing, giving support to the muscle action of the wings

Clawed fingers are supports for the feathers

To the modern eye, birds do not look like dinosaurs, despite their ancestry. The skeletons of birds have evolved over time, becoming much more lightweight than that of either *Compsognathus* or *Archaeopteryx*. This means that the modern bird needs to use much less energy to stay airborne. The heron is the modern bird whose shape perhaps most resembles *Compsognathus* and *Archaeopteryx*.

Tail is a short stump, with a fan of tail feathers

A typical bird, such as this heron, has lost some features that were common to *Compsognathus* and *Archaeopteryx*. It does not have hand claws, toothed jaws, or a bony tail because they would not help it to fly. Instead, the hand only supports the wing feathers, a lightweight horny beak has replaced the teeth, and the tail is a muscular stump controlling a broad surface of feathers.

HERON SKELETON

Upper foot bones fused into a single bone

ERA OF THE DINOSAURS

Dinosaurs roamed the planet for about 165 million years, during a time in the Earth's history called the Mesozoic Era. It is difficult to imagine how long this was, until we compare it with ourselves: humans have lived on Earth for less than two million years. During the Mesozoic Era, the Earth's landmasses changed dramatically, new seas were formed, and plants and animals evolved.

PRECAMBRIAN		4,600–545 million years ago (mya)
PALAEOZOIC ERA ("ANCIENT LIFE")	CAMBRIAN PERIOD	545–490 mya
	ORDOVICIAN PERIOD	490–445 mya
	SILURIAN PERIOD	445–415 mya
	DEVONIAN PERIOD	415–355 mya
	CARBONIFEROUS PERIOD	355–290 mya
	PERMIAN PERIOD	290–250 mya
MESOZOIC ERA ("MIDDLE LIFE")	TRIASSIC PERIOD	250–200 mya
	JURASSIC PERIOD	200–145 mya
	CRETACEOUS PERIOD	145–65 mya
CENOZOIC ERA ("RECENT LIFE")	TERTIARY PERIOD	65–1.64 mya
	QUATERNARY PERIOD	1.64 mya–present day

(DINOSAURS spans Triassic, Jurassic and Cretaceous periods)

▲ GEOLOGICAL TIMESCALE
Geologists divide Earth's long history into a series of time zones, from the origin of the planet, about 4,600 million years ago, right up to the present day. The major divisions are called eras. These are sub-divided into smaller time zones called periods. Within each period are smaller divisions called Ages (not shown in this diagram). Dinosaurs lived in the Mesozoic Era, which is divided into the Triassic, Jurassic and Cretaceous Periods. Humans live in the Quaternary Period of the Cenozoic Era.

TRIASSIC PERIOD: 250–200 MILLION YEARS AGO

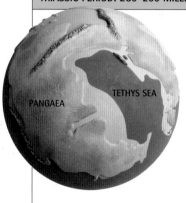

FOSSILIZED *RHYNCHOSAURUS*

TRIASSIC PLANET
In the Triassic Period all land was joined together as one great landmass. Scientists call this super-continent Pangaea, which means 'All Earth'.

TRIASSIC ANIMALS
The first dinosaurs lived in the early Triassic. Other reptiles also lived in this period, such as plant-eating rhynchosaurs. Fish and turtles swam in the sea, pterosaurs flapped their leathery wings in the sky, and the first mammals appeared.

JURASSIC PERIOD: 200–145 MILLION YEARS AGO

FOSSILIZED HORSESHOE CRAB

JURASSIC PLANET
Pangaea split into northern and southern landmasses in the Jurassic Period, divided by the ocean. In time, the two new continents moved apart.

JURASSIC ANIMALS
Dinosaurs colonized the land, from huge plant-eating species to smaller meat-eating ones. Pterosaurs ruled the sky, the first birds appeared, and icthyosaurs and horseshoe crabs swam in the seas.

CRETACEOUS PERIOD: 145–65 MILLION YEARS AGO

Mesozoic Era

CRETACEOUS PLANET
During the Cretaceous Period, Laurasia and Gondwana broke up into several smaller parts, beginning the formation of the continents we have today.

FOSSILIZED DRAGONFLY

FERN

FOSSILIZED GINKGO

Fossilized leaf is similar to the modern version

TRIASSIC PLANTS
Ferns, ginkgoes, and palm-like cycadeoids and cycads grew near streams. Scattered forests of conifers grew on drier lands. There was no grass, and there were no flowering plants. Inland areas were covered in hot, barren deserts with little or no plant life.

JURASSIC PLANTS
Coniferous forests covered vast areas of land. Ginkgoes, monkey puzzle trees, cycads, tall tree ferns, and giant horsetails were common. Ferns and mosses grew on the ground, but there were still no flowering plants or grass.

Perfect impression of a conifer leaf was preserved in this fossil

HORSETAIL

FOSSILIZED CONIFER SPRIG

MONKEY PUZZLE

CRETACEOUS ANIMALS
Fierce predatory dinosaurs hunted and scavenged for meat. Plant-eating dinosaurs grew body armour for protection. Crocodiles, turtles, and lizards flourished, and the first snakes appeared. Insects, birds, and pterosaurs flew in the sky, and small mammals ran on the ground.

Cones produced the earliest seeds

PINE WITH CONES

CRETACEOUS PLANTS
Flowering plants appeared, which were the ancestors of today's herbs, flowers, and broad-leaved trees. They became the main type of plant-life. Oak, maple, walnut, magnolia, and beech trees grew alongside the still abundant conifers, cycads, and tree ferns. There was still no grass.

BETULITES LEAF IN IRONSTONE NODULE

MAGNOLIA FLOWER

PASSION FLOWER

UP IN THE AIR

Soaring high above the land-living dinosaurs were the pterosaurs, which means "winged reptiles". The pterosaurs were relatives of dinosaurs, but they were not dinosaurs themselves. All had slim, hollow bones and wings made of skin that stretched between long finger-bones and the legs. Pterosaurs first appeared at the same time as the dinosaurs and lived alongside them until they too died out at the end of the Cretaceous Period. They were the supreme rulers of Earth's prehistoric skies, flapping their wings over land and sea.

Fur may have grown on their bodies

Beak was packed with many small teeth

PTERODACTYLUS ►

Pterodactylus was an agile flyer which probably fed on insects. Unlike other pterosaurs that had long tails, the tail of *Pterodactylus* was little more than a short, stubby point. Just 30 cm (12 in) long, it had a lightly built skeleton and thin, hollow bones. Perhaps these weight-saving features were designed to give *Pterodactylus* greater flight control, helping it to fly fast and giving it the ability to swoop and turn with ease.

Legs were short and probably had weak muscles

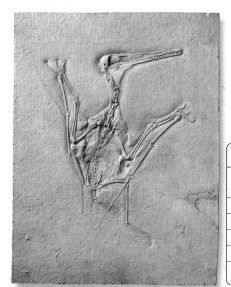

PTERODACTYLUS PROFILE

Pterodactylus belonged to the Pterodactyloid branch of the pterosaur family tree. These pterosaurs all had short tails.

Lived: 140 million years ago (Cretaceous)	
Habitat: rivers, seas, lakes	
Wingspan: up to 1.8 m (6 ft)	
Length: up to 30 cm (12 in)	
Diet: fish, insects	

▲ FOSSILIZED PTERODACTYLUS FEATURES
This fossil skeleton embedded in limestone shows *Pterodactylus*'s delicate skull and fine bones. The pterosaur's four fingers can be seen clearly. Three fingers on each of its hands were short and hook-like, and it is possible they were used for defence. The fourth finger can be seen here running diagonally from the hand on the right to the leg on the right. *Pterodactylus*'s wings were attached to each of these extremely long fingers and its legs.

Fibres inside the skin wings made them stiff

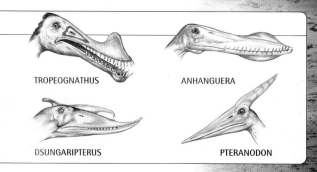

FLAMBOYANT HEADS

Several species of pterosaur sported crests on their heads and beaks. They were made from hard bone or soft tissue. It is not yet known if the crests were grown by males or females, or by both sexes. Their function is also uncertain. As the shape, size, and possibly the colour of crests differed between species, they may have helped pterosaurs recognize their own kind. They may also have been used in courtship displays or as stablilizers during flight.

TROPEOGNATHUS

ANHANGUERA

DSUNGARIPTERUS

PTERANODON

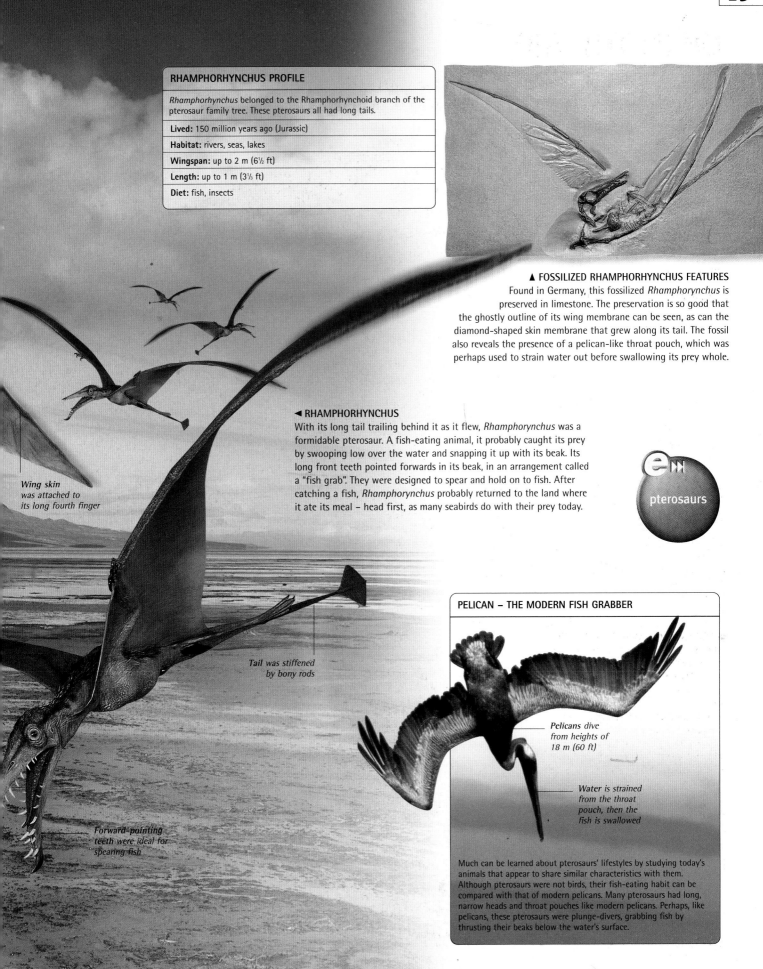

RHAMPHORHYNCHUS PROFILE

Rhamphorhynchus belonged to the Rhamphorhynchoid branch of the pterosaur family tree. These pterosaurs all had long tails.

Lived: 150 million years ago (Jurassic)	
Habitat: rivers, seas, lakes	
Wingspan: up to 2 m (6½ ft)	
Length: up to 1 m (3⅓ ft)	
Diet: fish, insects	

▲ FOSSILIZED RHAMPHORHYNCHUS FEATURES

Found in Germany, this fossilized *Rhamphorynchus* is preserved in limestone. The preservation is so good that the ghostly outline of its wing membrane can be seen, as can the diamond-shaped skin membrane that grew along its tail. The fossil also reveals the presence of a pelican-like throat pouch, which was perhaps used to strain water out before swallowing its prey whole.

◄ RHAMPHORHYNCHUS

With its long tail trailing behind it as it flew, *Rhamphorynchus* was a formidable pterosaur. A fish-eating animal, it probably caught its prey by swooping low over the water and snapping it up with its beak. Its long front teeth pointed forwards in its beak, in an arrangement called a "fish grab". They were designed to spear and hold on to fish. After catching a fish, *Rhamphorynchus* probably returned to the land where it ate its meal – head first, as many seabirds do with their prey today.

pterosaurs

Wing skin was attached to its long fourth finger

Tail was stiffened by bony rods

Forward-pointing teeth were ideal for spearing fish

PELICAN – THE MODERN FISH GRABBER

Pelicans dive from heights of 18 m (60 ft)

Water is strained from the throat pouch, then the fish is swallowed

Much can be learned about pterosaurs' lifestyles by studying today's animals that appear to share similar characteristics with them. Although pterosaurs were not birds, their fish-eating habit can be compared with that of modern pelicans. Many pterosaurs had long, narrow heads and throat pouches like modern pelicans. Perhaps, like pelicans, these pterosaurs were plunge-divers, grabbing fish by thrusting their beaks below the water's surface.

BELOW THE WAVES

While dinosaurs ruled the land, the ocean was the domain of many different families of marine reptiles, such as the nothosaurs, ichthyosaurs, pliosaurs, mosasaurs, and elasmosaurs. They were carnivores, preying on other sea creatures as well as each other. Although these reptiles spent their lives in water, they could not stay below the waves indefinitely. They breathed air, and had to swim to the surface to refill their lungs, before disappearing back into their underwater world.

marine reptiles

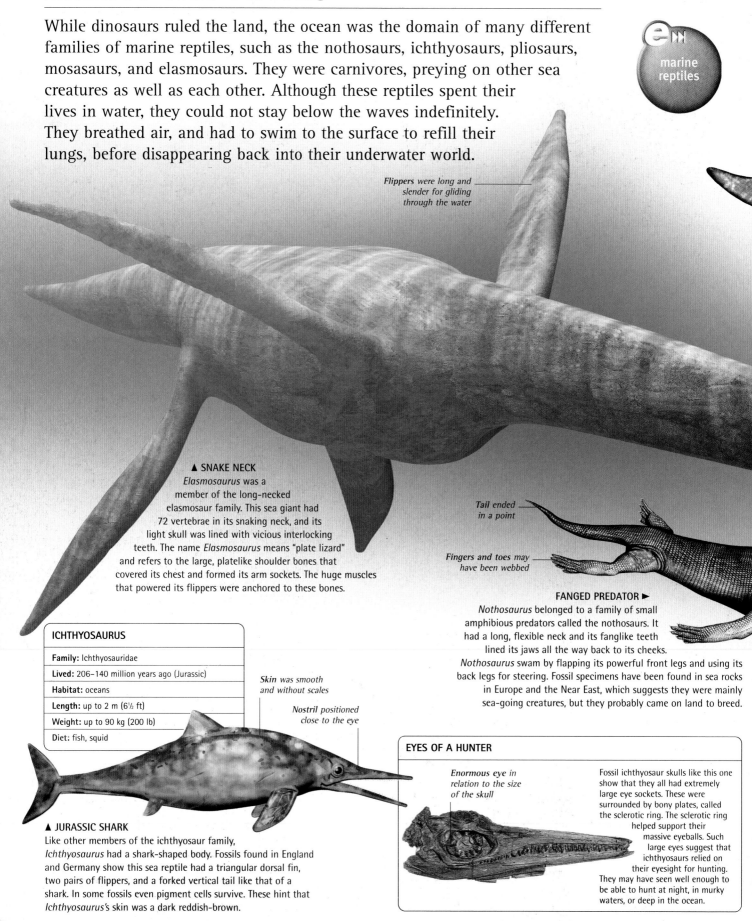

Flippers were long and slender for gliding through the water

▲ SNAKE NECK
Elasmosaurus was a member of the long-necked elasmosaur family. This sea giant had 72 vertebrae in its snaking neck, and its light skull was lined with vicious interlocking teeth. The name *Elasmosaurus* means "plate lizard" and refers to the large, platelike shoulder bones that covered its chest and formed its arm sockets. The huge muscles that powered its flippers were anchored to these bones.

Tail ended in a point

Fingers and toes may have been webbed

FANGED PREDATOR ▶
Nothosaurus belonged to a family of small amphibious predators called the nothosaurs. It had a long, flexible neck and its fanglike teeth lined its jaws all the way back to its cheeks. *Nothosaurus* swam by flapping its powerful front legs and using its back legs for steering. Fossil specimens have been found in sea rocks in Europe and the Near East, which suggests they were mainly sea-going creatures, but they probably came on land to breed.

ICHTHYOSAURUS	
Family: Ichthyosauridae	
Lived: 206–140 million years ago (Jurassic)	
Habitat: oceans	
Length: up to 2 m (6½ ft)	
Weight: up to 90 kg (200 lb)	
Diet: fish, squid	

Skin was smooth and without scales

Nostril positioned close to the eye

▲ JURASSIC SHARK
Like other members of the ichthyosaur family, *Ichthyosaurus* had a shark-shaped body. Fossils found in England and Germany show this sea reptile had a triangular dorsal fin, two pairs of flippers, and a forked vertical tail like that of a shark. In some fossils even pigment cells survive. These hint that *Ichthyosaurus*'s skin was a dark reddish-brown.

EYES OF A HUNTER

Enormous eye in relation to the size of the skull

Fossil ichthyosaur skulls like this one show that they all had extremely large eye sockets. These were surrounded by bony plates, called the sclerotic ring. The sclerotic ring helped support their massive eyeballs. Such large eyes suggest that ichthyosaurs relied on their eyesight for hunting. They may have seen well enough to be able to hunt at night, in murky waters, or deep in the ocean.

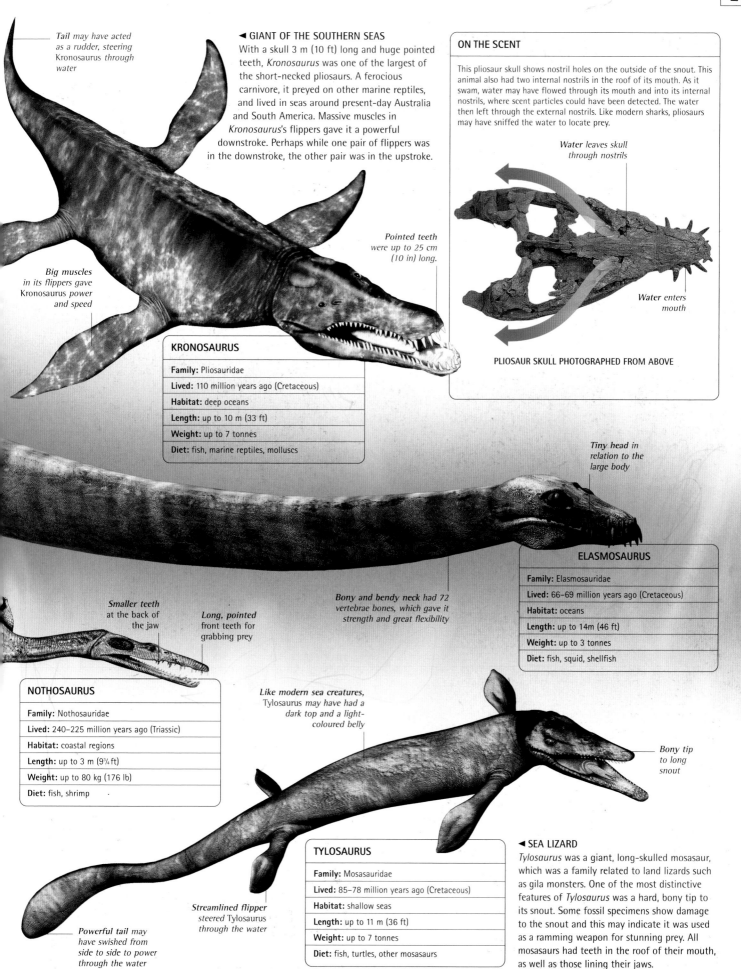

Tail may have acted as a rudder, steering Kronosaurus through water

◄ GIANT OF THE SOUTHERN SEAS

With a skull 3 m (10 ft) long and huge pointed teeth, Kronosaurus was one of the largest of the short-necked pliosaurs. A ferocious carnivore, it preyed on other marine reptiles, and lived in seas around present-day Australia and South America. Massive muscles in Kronosaurus's flippers gave it a powerful downstroke. Perhaps while one pair of flippers was in the downstroke, the other pair was in the upstroke.

ON THE SCENT

This pliosaur skull shows nostril holes on the outside of the snout. This animal also had two internal nostrils in the roof of its mouth. As it swam, water may have flowed through its mouth and into its internal nostrils, where scent particles could have been detected. The water then left through the external nostrils. Like modern sharks, pliosaurs may have sniffed the water to locate prey.

Water leaves skull through nostrils

Water enters mouth

PLIOSAUR SKULL PHOTOGRAPHED FROM ABOVE

Big muscles in its flippers gave Kronosaurus power and speed

Pointed teeth were up to 25 cm (10 in) long.

KRONOSAURUS

Family:	Pliosauridae
Lived:	110 million years ago (Cretaceous)
Habitat:	deep oceans
Length:	up to 10 m (33 ft)
Weight:	up to 7 tonnes
Diet:	fish, marine reptiles, molluscs

Tiny head in relation to the large body

Bony and bendy neck had 72 vertebrae bones, which gave it strength and great flexibility

ELASMOSAURUS

Family:	Elasmosauridae
Lived:	66–69 million years ago (Cretaceous)
Habitat:	oceans
Length:	up to 14m (46 ft)
Weight:	up to 3 tonnes
Diet:	fish, squid, shellfish

Smaller teeth at the back of the jaw

Long, pointed front teeth for grabbing prey

NOTHOSAURUS

Family:	Nothosauridae
Lived:	240–225 million years ago (Triassic)
Habitat:	coastal regions
Length:	up to 3 m (9¾ ft)
Weight:	up to 80 kg (176 lb)
Diet:	fish, shrimp

Like modern sea creatures, Tylosaurus may have had a dark top and a light-coloured belly

Bony tip to long snout

Powerful tail may have swished from side to side to power through the water

Streamlined flipper steered Tylosaurus through the water

TYLOSAURUS

Family:	Mosasauridae
Lived:	85–78 million years ago (Cretaceous)
Habitat:	shallow seas
Length:	up to 11 m (36 ft)
Weight:	up to 7 tonnes
Diet:	fish, turtles, other mosasaurs

◄ SEA LIZARD

Tylosaurus was a giant, long-skulled mosasaur, which was a family related to land lizards such as gila monsters. One of the most distinctive features of Tylosaurus was a hard, bony tip to its snout. Some fossil specimens show damage to the snout and this may indicate it was used as a ramming weapon for stunning prey. All mosasaurs had teeth in the roof of their mouth, as well as those lining their jaws.

DINOSAUR HABITATS

Not all the dinosaurs lived at the same time. Nor did they all live in the same part of the world. During the 180 million years that dinosaurs walked the Earth, the break-up of the supercontinent Pangaea and the resulting major changes of climate produced many different habitats. Continental drift changed the world's climate because it altered the flow of ocean currents and controlled how much of the world was covered in ice. Different dinosaurs evolved to live in different environments. Those that had existed on the dry Triassic supercontinent were quite different from those that lived on the scattered landmasses of the Cretaceous.

habitats

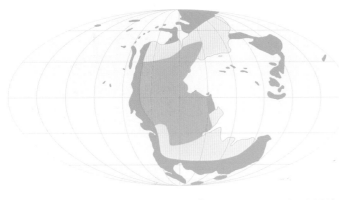

MAP KEY

▢ Desert
▢ Semi-desert
▢ Temperate forest

▲ TRIASSIC HABITATS (250–200 MILLION YEARS AGO)
During the Triassic, all the landmasses of the world were joined together, forming the single supercontinent, Pangaea. Because the continent was so huge, most inland areas were a long way from the ocean and there were extensive deserts. Only around the edges of the continent was there enough moisture for any vegetation. This was the time of the first dinosaurs and they lived everywhere.

MAP KEY

▢ Desert and semi-desert
▢ Temperate forest
▢ Tropical forest

▲ JURASSIC HABITATS (200–145 MYA)
By the Jurassic, Pangaea had begun to break up. Rift valleys produced long arms of ocean that reached into the depths of the continent, very like today's Red Sea in Egypt. Shallow seas spread across the lowlands and reached into the former deserts, giving rise to damper climates in most areas. There was much more vegetation than during the Triassic, although the plants were the same types.

HERRERASAURUS

PLATEOSAURUS

STEGOSAURUS

MAMENCHISAURUS

▲ RIVERSIDES
Plant and animal life was most common along the banks of rivers near the sea. The river banks were covered with ferns and the shallow water supported reed beds of horsetails. Early carnivorous dinosaurs such as *Herrerasaurus* hunted in these thickets.

▲ SCRUBLAND
The semi-desert supported a scrubby growth of plants that could tolerate a lack of water. The landscape must have looked rather like areas of southern Africa do today. The drought-resistant plants were browsed by early herbivores, such as the prosauropod *Plateosaurus*.

▲ RIPARIAN FOREST
As in the Triassic, the areas most covered by vegetation were by the riversides. Seasonal rainfall produced forests of tree ferns and ginkgoes, with an undergrowth of ferns and horsetails. These provided good feeding for herbivores such as *Stegosaurus*.

▲ DENSE CONIFEROUS FOREST
The forests were made up of primitive conifers such as monkey puzzles, cypresses, and podocarps (rare today), as well as relatives of the cycads. The tough needles on these evolved to guard against the intensive high browsing of sauropods such as *Mamenchisaurus*.

▲ MIXED FOREST

By the Cretaceous, flowering plants had begun to evolve. Dinosaurs with efficient chewing mechanisms, such as *Corythosaurus*, could both browse from trees and graze close to the ground. This led to the evolution of plants with seeds that could survive this treatment.

CORYTHOSAURUS

MAP KEY

☐ Desert and semi-desert

☐ Temperate forest

☐ Tropical forest

▲ CRETACEOUS HABITATS (145–65 MYA)

By the Cretaceous, the continents had broken apart, many of them beginning to look like the continents of today. The presence of so many different land areas meant that the climates were much more varied. The animal life was different on each continent as each group of animals evolved separately. So, for example, the dinosaurs of North America were different from those of South America.

SPINOSAURUS

EDMONTONIA

GALLIMIMUS

▲ SWAMPLAND

Swamps and river deltas are ideal places for the preservation of fossils. Steamy swamps existed along the edges of the Cretaceous continents. Wet-loving trees such as swamp cypresses dominated these areas. They provided the perfect habitat for fish-eating dinosaurs such as *Spinosaurus*.

▲ MOUNTAINS

Little is known about the vegetation of mountain habitats because most fossils come from lowland regions. But bones of armoured dinosaurs, such as *Edmontonia*, that look as though they have been washed down from mountain areas, have been found.

▲ DESERT PLAINS

The deserts supported some specialized animals. Although there was little to eat, a large number of different species of dinosaur lived in Cretaceous desert sandstones. The open vistas would have been ideal for long-legged running dinosaurs such as *Gallimimus*.

THE END OF THE DINOSAURS

About 65 million years ago, at the end of the Cretaceous Period, the Earth was affected by major changes to its environment. Animal and plant life were plunged into danger. It may only have taken one of these changes to affect life on Earth, or perhaps it was a combination of several. Whichever is the case, one thing is certain: dinosaurs became extinct at this time. Many theories exist to explain how dinosaurs died out.

extinction

DEATH FROM SPACE? ►
Earth is continually bombarded by debris from space, from specks of dust to lumps of rock. Most burn up as they pass through Earth's atmosphere, but some are big enough to survive. Space rocks that land on the Earth's surface are called meteorites. Did a large meteorite slam into the Earth, causing massive disruption that led to the death of the dinosaurs?

IMPACT CRATER ►
In the 1990s a meteorite crater 180 km (110 miles) across, on the seabed off the Yucatán Peninsula, Mexico, was dated to the late Cretaceous Period. The rock that made the Chicxulub crater was 10 km (6 miles) across. The impact may have made so much dust that the Sun's light was blotted out, leading to a mass extinction.

GULF OF MEXICO

PACIFIC OCEAN

OTHER DINOSAUR EXTINCTION THEORIES

DEATH FROM VOLCANOES?
Towards the end of the Cretaceous Period there were many volcanic eruptions in what is now central India. They were on a vast scale, blasting huge amounts of dust into Earth's atmosphere, where high winds blew them around the planet. As with the meteorite impact theory, this theory also says that atmospheric dust blotted out sunlight, sending the world into many years of cold and dark. With no sunlight, plants could not grow. With no food, animals starved and died.

DEATH FROM GIANT WAVES?
If a giant meteorite had splashed into the sea, it would have created a tsunami – a massive wave. Had it exploded on land, it would have made a shockwave big enough to trigger earthquakes and undersea landslides which could have unleashed megawaves. They would have raced at great speed towards land all around the globe. Within a few hours the waves might have pounded low-lying land, destroying habitats and disrupting Earth's plant and animal life.

DEATH FROM CLIMATE CHANGE?
As well as blasting dust into the atmosphere, volcanoes also create carbon dioxide – a poisonous gas that causes global warming. This extinction theory says that the rising levels of carbon dioxide caused a climate change known as the "greenhouse effect". Carbon dioxide prevented the Sun's heat from escaping back into space, so Earth's climate became hotter. Water evaporated. Plants withered and died. As animals lost their food sources, they died, too.

THE IMPACT THEORY: EXAMINING THE EVIDENCE

There is proof for the existence of the Chicxulub crater – but linking it to the death of the dinosaurs is harder to do. The first evidence for the crater came from boreholes that were made in the 1960s by a Mexican oil company, called Petrobas, which was exploring for oil in the Gulf of Mexico. Geologists noticed magnetic changes in the rocks they drilled into, and thought they had found volcanic rock. In the 1980s, Dr Luis Alvarez claimed that a meteorite could have triggered the death of the dinosaurs, and the hunt began to find a crater. Then, in 1990, geologists re-examining the Petrobas borehole records realized they were looking at a buried meteorite crater. Attention soon focused on the Chicxulub crater because it was formed about 65 million years ago - the same time the dinosaurs died out.

SEEING THE CHICXULUB CRATER
The Chicxulub crater lies partly beneath the Gulf of Mexico and partly on land. In this gravity map the white line is the coast of Mexico, above which is the sea. Even though half the crater is on the land, it is almost invisible to the eye as it is buried under layers of sediment. However, its circular outline becomes clear when changes in the region's magnetic field are plotted.

Close-up of a mineral from space found in ancient clay on Earth

Coin shows the thickness of the iridium-rich clay layer

LAYER THAT MARKS THE END OF THE DINOSAURS
The dark band in this photograph is clay containing iridium, a mineral found in meteorites. The iridium is thought to have got there after being blasted into the atmosphere following a meteorite impact. The band occurs worldwide, and was formed 65 million years ago – exactly the time when the dinosaurs died. It forms a boundary between rocks that have dinosaur fossils, and rocks that do not.

TURNING TO STONE

Most fossils are more than 10,000 years old, but many date back to the beginnings of life on Earth. Fossils are formed when animal or plant remains have been buried for millions of years. During this time, the remains change as minerals from the surrounding rock replace the minerals that make up the animal or plant. These changes happen so slowly that the remains keep their original shape. Most dinosaur skeletons are found in desert sandstones, after they have been buried by sandstorms, or in beds of rivers where river sand and mud have quickly covered them up.

fossils

Carbonized (turned to coal) leaves of the Jurassic fern Coniopteris

❶ DEATH IN A RIVER VALLEY
One day in the Late Triassic, a fleet-footed carnivore called *Coelophysis* lay down to die beside a river in Arizona, USA. It may have been sick or old, or it may have been attacked by a larger carnivore – we will never know. But 220 million years later, its remains have been unearthed by palaeontologists. An entire dinosaur skeleton can only survive as a fossil if it is buried immediately so that scavengers cannot tear it apart.

❷ BURIED IN SEDIMENT
The *Coelophysis* became buried in river mud and sand. After it was covered over, the flesh and soft organs rotted away and were washed out by water seeping through the sediments. Even though this skeleton was buried quickly in a river bed, the movements of the settling sand could have broken it up, pulling bone from bone and moving them about. The river current would have carried in more and more sediment, burying the skeleton deeper and deeper in the layers of sand and mud.

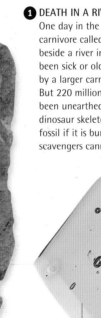

Amber

◀ PETRIFIED WOOD
A particularly detailed fossil is formed by a process called petrification. This happens when groundwater replaces bone or wood with a mineral such as silica. The cells of the bone or wood are gradually replaced, molecule by molecule, over millions of years. The resulting fossil, even though it may be made of silica, still has the cellular structure of the original, and allows scientists to examine its finest details.

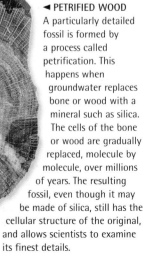

▲ FOSSILIZED FERN
Some fossils contain some of the original organic material. Leaves compressed in beds of shale or mudstone often decay slowly. They are made up of the elements carbon, hydrogen, and oxygen. The hydrogen and oxygen are lost to the air, but the carbon may be left as a thin film on the rock. These films are usually in the shape of the leaf. Fossilized plant material like this, piled up into thick beds, forms coal seams.

JEWELLED SPIDER ▲
Sometimes, although very rarely, a spider or some other small creature is preserved unaltered. This spider was trapped in the sticky resin seeping from the trunk of an ancient conifer. It was totally immersed, so no bacteria could reach it and it did not decay. The tree became buried and fossilized, and the resin changed into the mineral amber. The trapped creature is preserved complete.

Chamber of
ammonite shell cast

FOSSIL CASTS ▲

Sometimes a fossil rots away completely as the surrounding rock turns to stone. This may leave a hole, called a mould, in the rock in the exact shape of the fossil. If this mould is later filled with minerals, it forms a lump in the shape of the original called a cast. A beautiful cast forms when the natural spaces in an organism, such as the chambers of this ammonite shell, are filled with minerals.

Mould of fossil
of a 400-million-year-old starfish preserved in sandstone

PERFECT MOULDS ▲

When a fossil forms in a rock, it usually does so along the surface between two beds of the rock – the bedding plane. If the rock is split along this bedding plane, there may be part of the fossil on one piece of rock and part on the other. These two pieces of fossil are known as part and counterpart. Both are important to the palaeontologist, as together they will help reveal how the animal lived its life.

3 MINERALIZATION

As layers of sediment piled up, the layers at the bottom became compressed. The sand grains were wedged together, and water seeping through them left behind minerals. These minerals cemented the whole mass into a solid sedimentary rock. The groundwater also affected the skeleton of the now long-dead dinosaur. It destroyed the substance of the original bones, replacing it with minerals, just like the surrounding rock.

SABRE TOOTH ►

In more recent fossils, although the soft flesh and organs have disappeared, the hard parts of an animal – the shells, bones, or teeth – may have survived unchanged. Teeth are particularly hard as they are covered with enamel, and can survive even after the bones of the rest of the animal are lost. One survivor is this spectacular killing tooth of a sabre-toothed cat from the Cenozoic Era.

4 EXPOSED SKELETON

There the *Coelophysis* fossil may stay hidden forever, buried deep down where no-one can see it. But the rocks of the area are lifted up into a mountain range, and wind, frost, and rain begin to wear away the solid mass. The beds of rock crumble and wash away. Eventually, what is left of the skeleton is exposed at the surface. At this point, if it is not excavated, it too will be eroded away by the weather.

EARLY DISCOVERIES

Dinosaur fossils have been emerging from the rocks for millions of years, and people have been collecting them long before they knew what creatures they belonged to. In ancient China, dinosaur bones were believed to be the bones of dead dragons. It was not until 1841 that scientists recognized that huge reptiles had existed in the remote past. An eminent scientist of the time, Sir Richard Owen, declared this extinct group should be called Dinosauria.

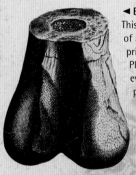

◄ BAFFLING BONE
This is the world's first picture of a dinosaur bone. It was printed in a book by Robert Plot in 1677. It baffled everyone at first – some people thought it belonged to a giant elephant. Scientists today know it was part of the thigh bone of the giant dinosaur *Megalosaurus*.

MEGALOSAURUS THIGH BONE

▼ A NEW WORD IS BORN
This picture shows the anatomist and palaeontologist Sir Richard Owen with an enormous extinct bird, called a moa. Owen was the first person to recognize dinosaurs as a distinct group, and he gave them their name in 1842. Combining the Greek words *deinos* ("terrible") and *sauros* ("lizard"), he created the word Dinosauria.

1822 Giant iguana

In 1822, Dr Gideon Mantell and his wife, Mary Ann, found some large teeth and bones near a quarry in Lewes, England. Dr Mantell concluded they belonged to a giant reptile, which he named *Iguanodon*.

GIDEON MANTELL

MARY ANN MANTELL

IGUANODON TOOTH

SECTION OF IGUANODON BACKBONE

MANTELL'S IGUANODON ►
Mantell's pen and ink sketch of *Iguanodon* shows how iguana-like he believed it to be. He based his ideas on the few bones that had been found, and on how living iguanas look. Mantell mistook *Iguanodon*'s thumb spike for a horn and placed it on its nose.

SKETCH OF IGUANODON

1824 First described

A specimen is recognized officially by scientists only when its description is published. The first person to describe and name a dinosaur was Dr William Buckland. In 1824, he published a description of an animal he called *Megalosaurus*.

WILLIAM BUCKLAND

▲ MEGALOSAURUS JAW
Buckland's work on *Megalosaurus* was based on the study of a fossil jaw much like this one. It had been housed in a museum in Oxford, England, since 1818. The size and shape suggested the jaw belonged to a giant reptile that was up to 12 m (40 ft) long. For this reason, Buckland gave the animal the name *Megalosaurus*, which means "big lizard".

fossil hunters

1853 First life-size models

In 1853, British sculptor Benjamin Waterhouse Hawkins teamed up with Richard Owen to build the first ever full-size dinosaur models. Using concrete, he created replicas of *Megalosaurus*, *Iguanodon*, and *Hylaeosaurus*.

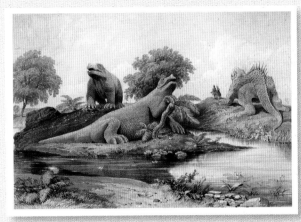

▲ MONSTERS IN THE PARK
In 1854, Hawkins' dinosaurs were installed in Sydenham Park, London, where they can still be found. His *Iguanodon* was so huge that a dinner party was held inside its hollow body. Hawkins also built dinosaurs for Central Park, New York, but they were broken up and buried in 1871.

1878 First skeletons

In 1878, coal miners in Bernissart, Belgium, found a giant fossil skeleton. Over the next three years, excavators managed to recover the skeletons of 32 *Iguanodon* from the mine. They were the first complete skeletons ever found.

A BERNISSART IGUANODON

▲ MOUNTED IN BRUSSELS
The Bernissart fossils were transported to Brussels for assembly and study by Louis Dollo, a scientist from the Royal Natural History Museum in Belgium. With several skeletons for comparison, he proved *Iguanodon* was two-legged, and the nose spike in Mantell's drawing was a thumb.

1860 First bird

In 1860, the impression of a feather was found in limestone in Bavaria, Germany. The next year, in the same area, the fossil of the earliest known bird was found. It was named *Archaeopteryx*, which means "ancient wing".

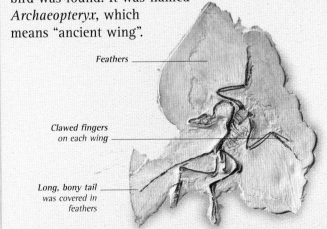

Feathers

Clawed fingers on each wing

Long, bony tail was covered in feathers

BAVARIAN BIRD ▲
The *Archaeopteryx* fossil was found in rocks which are 147 million years old. It shows this ancient bird was about the same size as a magpie. It had a mixture of reptilian and bird-like features, such as teeth and clawed fingers, as well as feathers and a wishbone.

1880s The Bone Wars

In the 1880s, the fierce rivalry between fossil hunters Marsh and Cope drove them to find and identify nearly 130 new North American dinosaurs. At the time, this battle of egos was known as the Bone Wars.

CHARLES OTHNIEL MARSH

EDWARD DRINKER COPE

NOT BRONTOSAURUS ►
Marsh named a new dinosaur *Apatosaurus* in 1877. In 1879 he used *Brontosaurus* for yet another discovery, whose nearly complete skeleton was mounted in Yale's Peabody Museum, USA. In 1903, it was found the two dinosaurs were the same species, so it is no longer called *Brontosaurus*. APATOSAURUS SKELETON

FOSSIL SITES

Dinosaurs lived all over the world, but their fossilized remains are not easy to find, or even, sometimes, to recognize. A desert surface free from vegetation, or the side of an eroding cliff, may expose fossils of dinosaurs buried in sediment millions of years ago. The remains may be incomplete, with many or most of the bones washed away by an ancient river. However, in nearly 200 years of painstaking exploration, palaeontologists have located many exciting dinosaur sites.

Excavating fossils in Utah

❶ UNITED STATES
In the Midwest and foothills of the Rocky Mountains are perhaps the most famous sites of all. In the Bone Wars of the 1880s, two US palaeontologists, Edward Drinker Cope and Charles Othniel Marsh, competed to find bigger and better dinosaur remains for the museums they represented. The result was that over a period of only 20 years, an incredible 150 new types of dinosaur were discovered.

❷ SOUTH AMERICA
Argentina and southern Brazil are the current hotbeds of palaeontological activity. The work being done there is showing what dinosaur life was like in the Cretaceous on the great southern continent of Gondwana, which included today's Africa and India. The fossil remains found in South America include some of the oldest – *Eoraptor* – as well as the largest of all the dinosaurs – the titanosaurs.

DISTRIBUTION ▶
A world map showing the distribution of dinosaur discoveries can give a misleading impression about the distribution of the dinosaurs themselves. Dinosaurs have not been excavated in all the places they lived in. There are many historical and political reasons for this – perhaps a team cannot reach an area because of war or because they are not welcome in a particular country. Also, the layout of the continents has changed since the Mesozoic Era – so we cannot tell exactly how many dinosaurs lived where.

fossil sites

❸ ISLE OF WIGHT
The first dinosaur remains to be discovered and correctly identified were in various parts of England in the 1820s. The long tradition of discovery is continued today on the Isle of Wight, off the south coast. Early Cretaceous theropods such as *Megalosaurus* and huge sauropods such as *Diplodocus* – dinosaurs previously associated with North America – have recently been excavated there.

SAHARA DESERT ❹

For more than 100 years, Africa has been a key destination for dinosaur-hunters. Deserts are ideal places to look for fossils and the Sahara Desert has revealed many. The first finds in Africa were made by expeditions from Germany before World War I began in 1914. Today, most of the excavations are being carried out in Morocco and Niger, and finds include the discovery of one of the largest carnivores ever found, *Carcharodontosaurus*.

Fossil of Ouranosaurus found in Niger

Parts of fossil skeleton buried in desert sand

KEY	
🔴	*Triassic sites*
⚪	*Jurassic sites*
🔴	*Cretaceous sites*

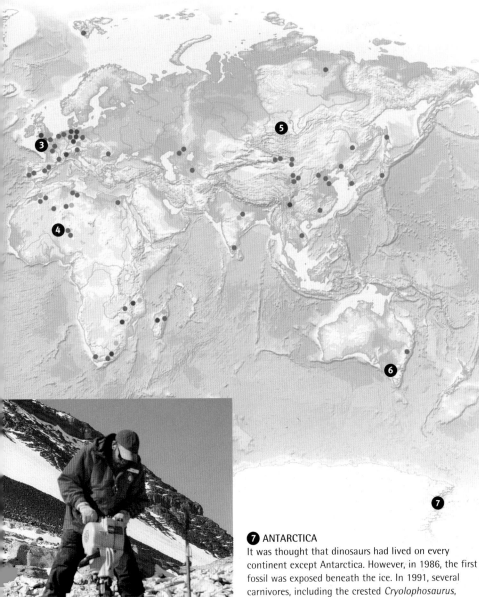

❺ GOBI DESERT

In the 1920s, expeditions led by the American Roy Chapman Andrews found dinosaur remains in the Gobi Desert in Mongolia. The original discoveries were made by accident – the first expedition was actually looking for the remains of early humans. The most exciting discoveries were the first dinosaur nests and eggs to be unearthed. Fossils are still being discovered there, mostly by teams from China, America, and Eastern Europe.

❼ ANTARCTICA

It was thought that dinosaurs had lived on every continent except Antarctica. However, in 1986, the first fossil was exposed beneath the ice. In 1991, several carnivores, including the crested *Cryolophosaurus*, were found on Mount Kirkpatrick. There have been other finds since. In early Jurassic times, when these animals lived, Antarctica was part of the supercontinent Pangaea, and was much closer to the Equator.

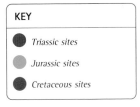

❻ AUSTRALIA

There have been several dinosaur discoveries in Australia, but the most important were made in the 1970s. The site, on the coast of Victoria, has since been named Dinosaur Cove. The finds there show that ornithopods were abundant in this area in the Cretaceous, when the land was within the Antarctic Circle. The remains of these dinosaurs show that they had adapted to long Antarctic winters of intense cold.

IN THE FIELD

In the past, dinosaur digs were very different from what they are today. Fragile fossils were broken by crude digging methods, and even more were shaken to pieces on their way to museums. Records were rarely kept of fossil sites. As a result, valuable specimens and information have been lost for ever. Modern excavation involves studying both the skeleton and its surroundings. Like detectives, palaeontologists examine the site for clues about the dinosaur's life. Then the fossils are carefully removed and prepared for transportation.

Leg bones are quite complete

excavation

Toe bones have been scattered but are identifiable

❶ PREPARING THE SITE
When a dinosaur skeleton is discovered, the first thing to do is remove the rock and soil above the layer in which the specimen lies. At this site, at Judith River in Montana, USA, 6 m (20 ft) of material, known as overburden, was removed with bulldozers and explosives. The last 1 m (3 ft) of material was removed with hand tools, such as hammers and chisels, until only a thin layer was left over the skeleton.

❷ EXPOSING THE FOSSIL
The rock that the fossil is embedded in is called the matrix. This is removed with great care, usually by hand, using fine chisels, brushes, and dental tools. Sometimes the fossilized bones are quite hard and the matrix is loose, crumbly, and easy to clear away. But often the fossil bones and rock have equal hardness, which makes the job more difficult.

❸ MAPPING THE SITE
The next task is to record exactly where each specimen lies. To do this accurately, a grid of wire or strings is placed over the site to divide it into smaller areas. Everything is photographed, as well as drawn. The mapping covers not only the skeleton, but all the other fossils that lie in the same bed of rock. These might provide useful details about the behaviour of the dinosaur, or how it died.

❹ SITE MAP
A map of the site is drawn up showing the position of all the bones. Every piece is catalogued and numbered so it can be identified later when the skeleton is studied in the laboratory. Anything else of interest, such as other fossils or sedimentary structures, is also marked on the map.

▼ EXPOSED FOSSIL

As the skeleton is exposed, palaeontologists get a clearer picture of what the specimen is. They are able to identify the parts of the animal and can estimate how complete it is. These are the bones of a hadrosaur called *Brachylophosaurus*. It is lying on its side, with its skull twisted back over its spine. At this stage, it is important to work as quickly as possible, as newly exposed fossils are very vulnerable to the weather.

Backbone appears to end abruptly — the tail is either missing, or is still to be uncovered

Spinal column (back bone) is still together

Skull has broken up and the pieces are scattered

Front limbs were less powerful than the back ones

▲ LIFT OFF

Fossils must be extremely carefully packed so that they are not damaged on their way to the museum or laboratory. Sites are often in very remote areas and the journey can be long and bumpy. Fossils have been known to travel in jeeps, planes, boats, trucks, and even horse-drawn carts. On major excavations, helicopters are sometimes used to transport very delicate specimens.

Strong cable lifts fossil bones in their plaster jacket — some blocks weigh several tonnes

❺ INNER DRESSING

Many fossils are very fragile and, before they can be removed and transported, they need to be carefully prepared. First, the fossil is sprayed or painted with a glue or resin that seeps into it and solidifies. This makes the fossil harder. Next it is covered in a protective layer of paper or foil, and wrapped in bandages.

❻ PLASTER FIELD JACKET

The top of the bone is then covered with runny plaster. When this has set hard, the underside of the fossil can be dug out. It is then turned over and covered in bandages and plaster, so that the whole thing is enclosed in a solid plaster jacket. The fossil is now ready to be packed in a crate and taken to a laboratory.

BODY FOSSILS

Palaeontologists can have a hard time finding and identifying dinosaur fossils because they are usually embedded in stone. Usually, only the hard parts of the animal have been fossilized, and even then, a complete skeleton is rare – isolated bones and teeth are more common. Now and again, however, particularly good fossils are unearthed: fossils of complete skeletons in their living position, fossil skin textures, or very occasionally, indications of soft anatomy. Rare though these finds are, there have been enough of them over the past two centuries to allow scientists to build up a good picture of how dinosaurs lived.

fossils

Tail chevrons (V-shaped bones) are still in place

Long whip-like tail

Bones of left leg are missing

Leg bones flexed in the living position

Right leg is missing its foot

Long finger bones for grasping plant food

MUMMIFIED DINOSAURS

Dinosaur "mummies" have been created after dead dinosaurs were washed into a river and lay in soft mud before they decayed. The soft mud takes the impression of the skin texture and this is preserved when the mud solidifies to stone. These skin impressions are immensely valuable because they give scientists an idea of what the outer covering of a dinosaur would have looked like. However, they can also be misleading. For decades, the shrivelled skin of one hadrosaur's hand gave rise to the idea that the fingers were webbed and that the hadrosaurs were swimming animals. Dry heat has made the tendons of this *Edmontosaurus* carcass shrink. Found in Wyoming, USA, the body gave scientists the first evidence that dinosaur skin was similar to that of today's reptiles.

Shrivelled remains of weight-bearing pad, looking like webbed fingers

Impression of dried skin stretched tightly over rib cage

EDMONTOSAURUS CARCASS

Body is twisted because shrinking tendons have pulled on the bones

Head pulled right back

Neck folded back on shoulders

▲ ALMOST COMPLETE SKELETON

This *Heterodontosaurus* is a palaeontologist's dream! A nearly complete dinosaur skeleton, still articulated (with its joints in position), and in the pose of a living animal is an unusual find. It is possible to imagine this rabbit-sized plant-eater skipping along, head up and alert, tail swinging out behind. Unfortunately, a skeleton as well preserved as this is very rare. Usually, the bones are pulled apart and scattered by animals, bad weather, or flowing water. Most dinosaur fossils are fragments of bones or incomplete skeletons. The skull is so lightweight that it has nearly always collapsed into shards or is missing altogether.

◄ DINOSAUR TOOTH

Teeth are particulary hard and last well. They are covered in a substance called enamel that makes them even harder than bone. Teeth may fossilize when the bone of the animal is lost. Often the teeth are all that is found of a dinosaur, and some species are known from their teeth alone. The carnivorous theropods shed their teeth and grew new ones throughout their lives, so theropod teeth, such as those of the dinosaur *Megalosaurus*, are common.

DAMAGED
MEGALOSAURUS
TOOTH

BRACHYLOPHOSAURUS
SKULL

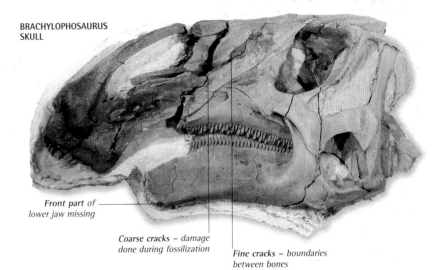

Front part of lower jaw missing

Coarse cracks – damage done during fossilization

Fine cracks – boundaries between bones

FRACTURED SKULL ▲

Skulls of dinosaurs are not often found by palaeontologists. The skull is made up of many different sections all joined together, and soon after death most skulls come apart. Each side of a skull has about a dozen individual bones and, not counting the teeth, each lower jaw has three – four in the ornithischians. This hadrosaur skull, even though it is broken and parts of it are missing, is still a valuable find and has helped the palaeontologists understand the dinosaur better. Many dinosaur skeletons have been found that are almost complete but lack the skull – arguably the most important part of the animal's anatomy.

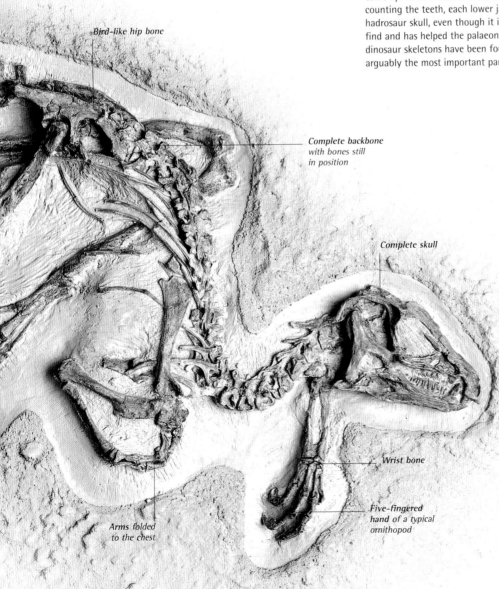

Bird-like hip bone

Complete backbone with bones still in position

Complete skull

Wrist bone

Five-fingered hand of a typical ornithopod

Arms folded to the chest

DINOSAUR HEART ▲

The rarest fossil find of all is that of an internal organ. The digestive system, lungs, heart, and all the other soft parts usually rot away quickly and leave nothing that can fossilize. Now and again, however, there is a lucky find. This fossil skeleton of the ornithopod *Thescelosaurus* was unearthed in the USA in 1997. Just below the shoulder blade, which is the large bone running from top left down to centre right, there is a round mineralized lump in the centre of the picture. This may well be a fossilized dinosaur heart – the first ever to be found.

TRACE FOSSILS

Some of the most interesting fossils contain nothing of the dinosaur itself. They are simply the marks the animal left behind as it walked along and take the form of footprints, skin impressions, or even its droppings. Fossils like this are called trace fossils and can be very useful as they give scientists an insight into how the dinosaur lived. Nests and eggs also provide useful indications of a dinosaur's lifestyle. It is usually easier to identify a particular dinosaur from a nest or a fossilized egg than from a trace fossil.

SKIN PRINT ▲
Finding an impression of dinosaur skin is rare but very exciting for the palaeontologist. A trace fossil of skin may happen when a dinosaur has lain or sat down in a muddy hollow. The mud, along with the impression, is later buried and turned to stone. More often, skin survives as a fossil when a dinosaur has been buried shortly after death, skin intact. The skin decays away, but the surrounding mud has already taken an impression.

Three-toed footprint in sandstone

◄ FOOTPRINTS
The most common type of trace fossils is footprints. Fossil tracks are sometimes more common than the animal's body fossils. A dinosaur will leave only one dead body, but perhaps millions of footprints. They show how the animal walked, whether it lived alone or with others, and even whether or not it dragged its tail on the ground. However, it is always hard to match a footprint to a particular species.

COPROLITES ▲
Coprolites are the fossilized droppings of animals, identified by where they are found – for example, near a species' nest. These fossils can reveal a lot about the diet of the animal that formed them. Coprolites from a tyrannosaur may contain bits of hadrosaur bone. A hadrosaur's coprolites may contain undigested plant material, including identifiable spores and pollen. The shape of a coprolite can also tell us about the shape of a dinosaur's intestines.

THE MAKING OF A DINOSAUR TRACK

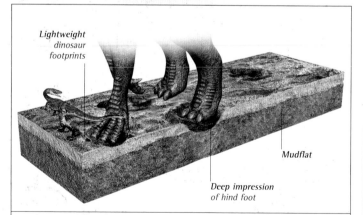

Lightweight dinosaur footprints
Mudflat
Deep impression of hind foot

MAKING FOOTPRINTS
Fossil footprints can mislead scientists. In this scene, a four-footed dinosaur walks across a mudflat and a smaller dinosaur scampers by. The hind feet of the larger dinosaur are heavy enough to press through the top layer of wet mud into the firmer layer that lies underneath. The front feet of the larger dinosaur and those of the little dinosaur leave impressions only on the surface layer.

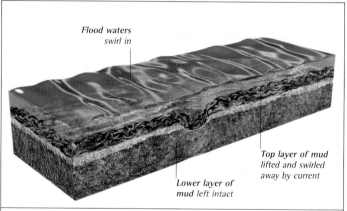

Flood waters swirl in
Top layer of mud lifted and swirled away by current
Lower layer of mud left intact

THE SURFACE IS FLOODED
Shortly after the footprints are made and the animals have moved on, the mudflat is flooded when the nearby river overflows its banks. The turbulent water current sweeps away the soft top layer of the mud, carrying with it and destroying the shallow prints of the larger dinosaur's front feet and those of the little two-footer. It does not touch the firmer layer of mud that lies underneath.

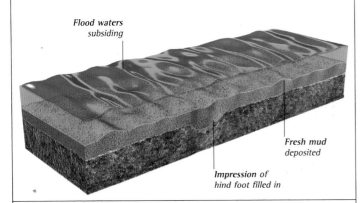

▲ DINOSAUR NEST

This fossilized nest was found in Montana, USA, in the 1980s. At first, scientists thought that it was the nest of a hypsilophodont called *Orodromeus*, because bones of *Orodromeus* were found scattered all around. It is now known that this is the nest of a carnivore called *Troodon*. It had probably been feeding its family on *Orodromeus* that it had caught. Each egg in a *Troodon* nest was embedded upright in mud to keep it warm, with only the top exposed to the air.

fossils

Reconstructed eggshell

Head of baby tucked down between legs

EGG FOSSIL ►

It was clear what kind of dinosaur the nest belonged to when the eggs were cut open and examined. The fossilized bones inside were those of a baby *Troodon*. Many dinosaur eggs are fossilized in such detail that the microscopic structure of the egg shell can be seen. From this type of detail, it is possible to tell that dinosaur egg shells were hard, like those of a bird, rather than soft and leathery, like those of a lizard or crocodile.

Fossilized shell fragments

Impression of the left leg bones

MICROSCOPIC VIEW OF A
DINOSAUR EGGSHELL

Bones of left leg folded up against the chest

▲ INSIDE THE EGG

From the bones found fossilized inside the egg, it is possible to make a reconstruction of the baby *Troodon* as it got ready to hatch. Its head is tucked down between its legs. The head and eyes are large, as is usual with baby animals. There is also a horn on the nose that it would have used to break out from the inside through the tough shell. This horn would have been lost soon after the animal hatched.

Flood waters subsiding

Fresh mud deposited

Impression of hind foot filled in

SEDIMENTATION CONTINUES

After the flood water subsides, the disturbed mud from the top layer settles once more in a different place. More mud is carried in by the waters flowing over the top, and this covers the whole area and fills in the impression left by the large dinosaur's hind feet. Later floods deposit more and more mud on top. Eventually, all these mud layers are compressed and, over time, become solidified into sedimentary rock.

No impressions of front feet or smaller dinosaur

Convex impression of hind feet

200 MILLION YEARS LATER

Eventually, the sedimentary rock is exposed at the surface. If the rock is split along the right layer, the footprints appear. The upper layer is often better preserved than the lower layer, and the prints of the hind feet show in 3-D. It can look as if only one big bipedal dinosaur has passed by.

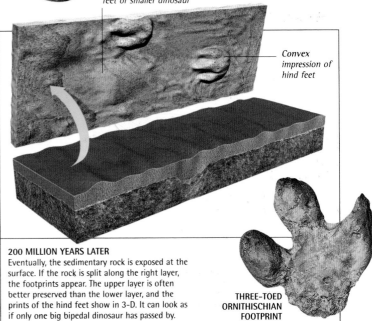

THREE-TOED
ORNITHISCHIAN
FOOTPRINT

EXAMINING FOOTPRINTS

It has been said that the footprints of a dinosaur can tell us more about the dinosaur than its skeleton. This is because footprints are a record of the living, moving animal, while the skeleton is simply the remains of its dead body. The footprints of any animal can tell you a number of things about it, such as its size, and how it stood, ran, or walked. By comparing footprints with dinosaur skeletons, scientists are able to get a clearer picture of what dinosaurs were really like. A set of tracks can reveal more about dinosaur behaviour, and can even give an idea of its speed. Some of the largest footprints are made by brontosaurs. These can be over 1 m (3 ft) long and 0.7 m (2 ft) across.

FOOTPRINT LENGTH

FOOTPRINT WIDTH

LEFT PRINT

MEASURING TRACKWAYS ▲

When analysing trackways, such as these *Iguanodon* footprints, many different measurements are taken. The length and width of the footprint, and the trackway width, can tell us about the dinosaur's size. The trackway width can also reveal the dinosaur's stance. Other measurements such as pace length (distance between successive footprints), stride length (distance between prints made by the same foot), and the angle between the prints of alternate feet (pace angulation), can tell us how the animal moved.

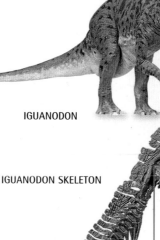

IGUANODON

IGUANODON SKELETON

Hip height

Foot length

▲ INDICATORS OF BEHAVIOUR

These tracks in Arizona, USA, were made by agile, meat-eating ceratosaurs called *Dilophosaurus*, which ran on two legs. A set of footprints like this can give an idea of how the animal that made them behaved. A single line of footprints suggests a loner, while several parallel trackways may mean the animal lived as part of a herd. Occasionally, we find trackways of large and small footprints together, from dinosaurs that lived in a family group. Trackways can also show carnivorous dinosaurs pursuing prey.

▲ CALCULATING DIMENSIONS

The size of a dinosaur can be worked out from its footprint. The key measurement is the height of the hip, which is usually estimated as about four times the length of the footprint. If there is a set of prints, it should be possible to tell whether the dinosaur walked on two legs or four, and to get a more accurate idea of the size and shape of the animal, and how it stood and moved. *Iguanodon* was 8–12 m (26–40 ft) long, and probably walked with its body held horizontally.

COMPARING THE STANCE OF ANIMALS

If dinosaurs were like most modern reptiles, you would expect them to stand with their limbs sticking out from the sides of the body, and elbows and knees bent at right angles. This is called the sprawling stance. Or you might imagine that they walked in a semi-sprawling stance, with elbows and knees slightly bent, like modern crocodiles. However, fossil footprints are too close together to have been produced by either stance. They show that dinosaurs walked upright, like modern mammals, with vertical legs directly below the body, and supporting its weight. This erect stance was crucial to the survival of the dinosaurs. It meant that many were swift and agile on land. Also, because they did not need to use energy supporting their bodies, they were able to be very active — looking for food, for example.

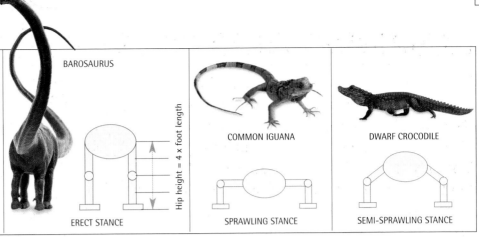

BAROSAURUS

Hip height = 4 x foot length

ERECT STANCE

COMMON IGUANA

SPRAWLING STANCE

DWARF CROCODILE

SEMI-SPRAWLING STANCE

RUNNING AND WALKING SPEEDS

How fast were the dinosaurs? We cannot be sure. It is only possible to estimate the speeds achieved by dinosaurs. Figures have been produced using mathematical calculations based on trackway measurements, leg length, weight, and several other measurements. But there are unknown factors, such as the strength of the leg bones, and the uncertainty of whether or not the dinosaurs were warm blooded – these would affect the calculations and mean that the results cannot be reliable. A few estimated speeds are shown in this chart.

WALK large sauropod
WALK small sauropod
WALK large theropod
RUN small theropod
RUN small theropod
RUN ornithopod
FAST RUN small theropod
SPRINT human athlete
FAST RUN ostrich
FAST RUN racehorse

0 kph	4	8	12	13	17	36	40	54	61
(0 mph)	(2)	(5)	(7)	(8)	(11)	(22)	(25)	(34)	(40)

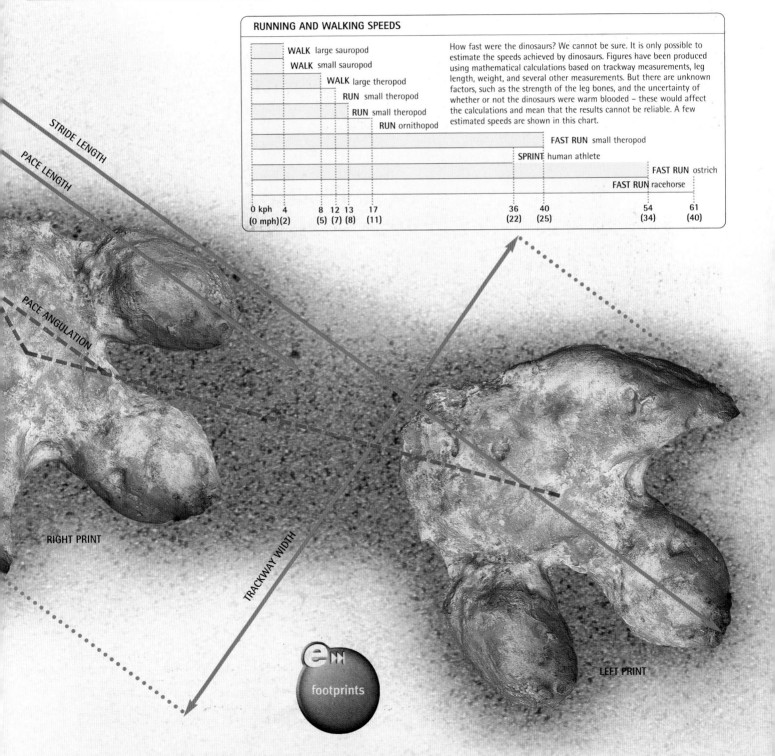

STRIDE LENGTH

PACE LENGTH

PACE ANGULATION

RIGHT PRINT

TRACKWAY WIDTH

LEFT PRINT

footprints

IN THE LAB

When a fossil arrives in a laboratory, it is usually embedded in a chunk of the rock it was found in. The first job for the specially trained technicians, called preparators, is to free the fossil from the rock and clean it up. Sometimes they can remove the rock from the fossil with chemicals. The fossil is left in a bath of acid for several months while the rock around the fossil, called the matrix, dissolves. Preparators also repair bones, strengthen any weak parts with glues and resins, and may make missing bones if the skeleton is to be reconstructed.

preparation

Preparation is very time-consuming work. The *Tyrannosaurus* skeleton in the Field Museum in Chicago, USA, for example, took 12 people a total of 25,000 hours to complete.

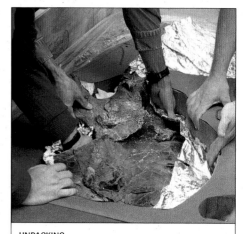

UNPACKING
Technicians at the Field Museum in Chicago, USA, open the carefully packed crates of bones from a *Tyrannosaurus* skeleton — here a hip bone. Although the sex of the dinosaur is not known, the team have named it Sue, after the woman who discovered it.

REMOVING THE FIELD JACKET
First the plaster jacket that protected the fossil in transport is taken off. Here a preparator is using a cast-cutting saw to cut carefully through the jacket on some of Sue's backbones. Beneath the plaster is a layer of protective foil or paper, which is also removed.

PNEUMATIC DRILL
A range of tools are used to clean up the fossil. Here a preparator uses a pneumatic drill to break up the main body of rock around the fossil. He wears a mask so that he does not breathe in any rock dust. At this stage, pieces of rock are removed in quite large pieces.

FINE CLEANING
Finer cleaning is done with a pen-shaped device, called a scribe, which crumbles the rock using high-frequency vibrations. This technician is working on one of Sue's 58 teeth, the largest of which were 30 cm (1 ft) long. Over 3,500 hours were spent working on Sue's skull.

AIR ABRASION
Another method of fine cleaning is to shoot baking soda at the specimen in powerful blasts of air. This is called air abrasion. Very detailed cleaning is sometimes carried out under a microscope with dental tools. Broken bones can now be repaired using special glues and adhesives.

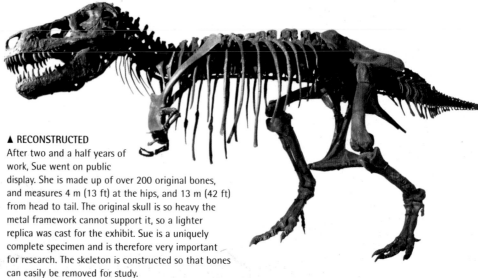

▲ RECONSTRUCTED
After two and a half years of work, Sue went on public display. She is made up of over 200 original bones, and measures 4 m (13 ft) at the hips, and 13 m (42 ft) from head to tail. The original skull is so heavy the metal framework cannot support it, so a lighter replica was cast for the exhibit. Sue is a uniquely complete specimen and is therefore very important for research. The skeleton is constructed so that bones can easily be removed for study.

COMPUTER RECONSTRUCTION

Today computers are used in all aspects of dinosaur study. In the field, fossil sites can be mapped and plotted using electronic measuring devices. In the laboratory, techniques such as computer reconstruction enable palaeontologists to create dinosaurs from fossils on screen, and study them as never before – inside and out.

DINOSAUR ON SCREEN ▶

If doctors want to look inside the human body, they can do this by creating a Computerized Axial Tomography (CAT) scan. This involves taking X-rays of the patient from many angles, putting the results into a computer, and building up a 3-D image of the patient's insides. This technique can be used to look inside dinosaur fossils too, and has produced images of the insides of dinosaur bones and inside dinosaur eggs, for example. Here a palaeontologist compares a CAT scan of the brain of a *Tyrannosaurus*, taken from a fossil, with a drawing of another *Tyrannosaurus* brain.

Crushed snout as the top and bottom parts of the skull have smashed together

▲ COMPRESSED SKULL

This is a 3-D image of a flattened skull of a *Tyrannosaurus* from the Field Museum in Chicago, USA. The image can be turned to show both sides, and cut in half to reveal the shape of the bones inside. This allows scientists to take a virtual journey through the skull of a dinosaur. To create this image, the skull was scanned for 500 hours by a specialist X-ray machine normally used to detect hidden flaws in jet engines and Space Shuttle parts.

Skull is expanded vertically to show the original proportions of the skull

▼ REBUILT IN 3-D

When a fossil is found it is usually crushed and distorted by the pressure of sediment and rock over millions of years. However, the image produced by a CAT scan can be manipulated to undo any damage to the specimen. In this image, the flattened skull of the *Tyrannosaurus* has been pulled out to show what it would have looked like before it was deformed, with bones shown in their proper proportions and positions. Although the brain of the *Tyrannosaurus* did not become fossilized, the braincase surrounding it was well preserved, giving scientists a good picture of the brain itself. It is likely *Tyrannosaurus* had a good sense of smell, as half of its brain appears to be dedicated to interpreting smells.

Skull's shape and size show Sue's brain was 30 cm (1 ft) long

Cheeks are expanded horizontally to reverse the effects of crushing

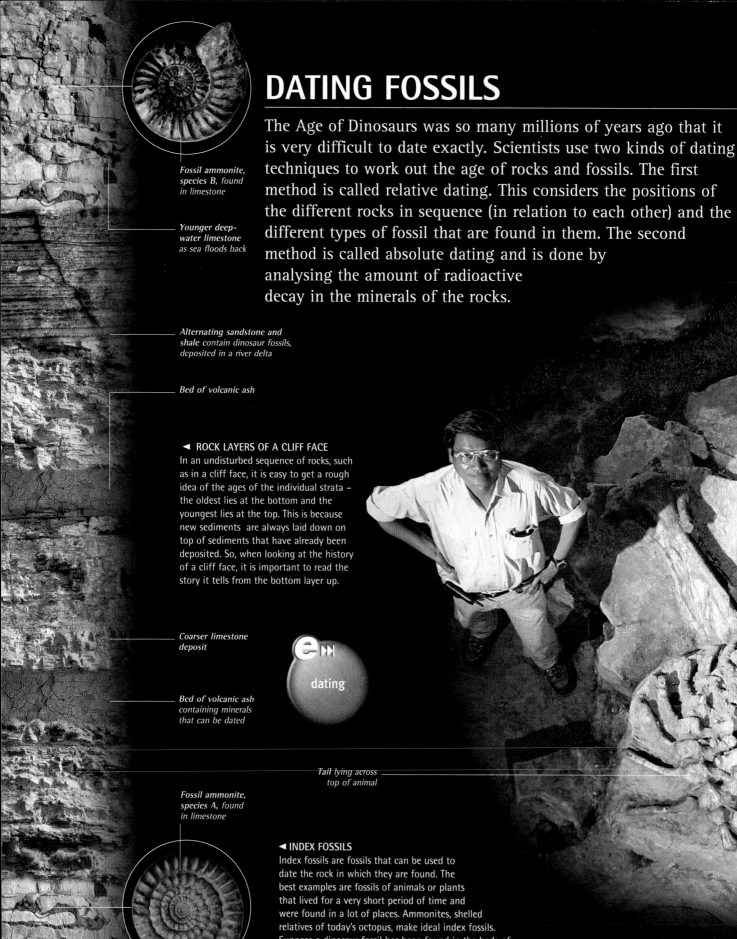

DATING FOSSILS

The Age of Dinosaurs was so many millions of years ago that it is very difficult to date exactly. Scientists use two kinds of dating techniques to work out the age of rocks and fossils. The first method is called relative dating. This considers the positions of the different rocks in sequence (in relation to each other) and the different types of fossil that are found in them. The second method is called absolute dating and is done by analysing the amount of radioactive decay in the minerals of the rocks.

Fossil ammonite, species B, found in limestone

Younger deep-water limestone as sea floods back

Alternating sandstone and shale contain dinosaur fossils, deposited in a river delta

Bed of volcanic ash

◄ ROCK LAYERS OF A CLIFF FACE
In an undisturbed sequence of rocks, such as in a cliff face, it is easy to get a rough idea of the ages of the individual strata – the oldest lies at the bottom and the youngest lies at the top. This is because new sediments are always laid down on top of sediments that have already been deposited. So, when looking at the history of a cliff face, it is important to read the story it tells from the bottom layer up.

Coarser limestone deposit

e ►►
dating

Bed of volcanic ash containing minerals that can be dated

Tail lying across top of animal

Fossil ammonite, species A, found in limestone

◄ INDEX FOSSILS
Index fossils are fossils that can be used to date the rock in which they are found. The best examples are fossils of animals or plants that lived for a very short period of time and were found in a lot of places. Ammonites, shelled relatives of today's octopus, make ideal index fossils. Suppose a dinosaur fossil has been found in the beds of an ancient delta (the mouth of a river leading to the sea). The sediment of this area was laid down after ammonite A appeared 199 million years ago, and before ammonite B became extinct 195 million years ago. This narrows the date of the delta beds to the four million years between these dates.

Deep-water limestone formed at bottom of the sea

Fossil of Phuwiangosaurus *found in layers of sandstone and shale*

Fossils in surrounding rock are also gathered for analysis

▼ DATING A DINOSAUR SKELETON

Scientists find out the age of a dinosaur fossil by dating not only the rocks in which it lies, but those below and above it. This *Phuwiangosaurus* was the first fossil dinosaur found in Thailand, and it is known that it lived in the Cretaceous because of other fossils found nearby. Sometimes, scientists already know the age of the fossil because fossils of the same species have been found elsewhere and it has been possible to establish accurately from those when the dinosaur lived. Geologists call this the principle of lateral continuity. A fossil will always be younger than fossils in the beds beneath it and this is called the principle of superposition.

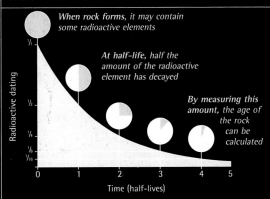

RADIOMETRIC DATING

When rock forms, it may contain some radioactive elements

At half-life, half the amount of the radioactive element has decayed

By measuring this amount, the age of the rock can be calculated

Radioactive dating (y-axis: ½, ½, ¼, ⅛, ⅟₁₆)
Time (half-lives) (x-axis: 0 1 2 3 4 5)

There are some radioactive elements in rock that decay by giving off energy and turning into different, more stable elements. This radioactive decay takes place at a constant rate for each radioactive element. Scientists know exactly how long it will take for half the quantity of the element to change, and this state is known as its half-life. After another half-life has passed, the element will have decayed to a quarter of its original amount. After another half-life has passed, it will have decayed to an eighth, and so on.

A good example of this is potassium-argon dating. The half-life of potassium-40 is 1,310 million years, after which half of its substance will have changed into stable argon-40.

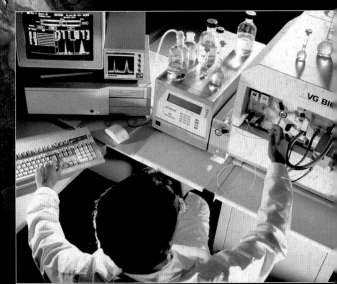

▲ ABSOLUTE DATING

By looking at the layers of volcanic ash in a sedimentary sequence, it is possible to work out the exact time of an ancient volcanic eruption. Scientists do this by using radiometric dating in a laboratory to analyse the minerals created by the eruption. The two beds of volcanic ash in the cliff face on the left are dated at 197 and 196 million years respectively. The dinosaur bed is above these, so it is younger. By combining this knowledge with what is known about the ammonites, it is possible to date the dinosaur fossil at 196 or 195 million years old.

Bones are still articulated (in position), showing that the burial took place suddenly

RECONSTRUCTING THE PAST

Reconstructing a dinosaur skeleton is a complex job as usually only a fraction of the skeleton is recovered. Palaeontologists assume the missing pieces will resemble those of the animal's closest relatives, and use these as guides for making replacement parts. Most excavated fossils are too delicate to put back together, so technicians construct a lightweight replica of the skeleton, which is then erected in a life-like pose. Rearing on its hind legs, the American Museum of Natural History's *Barosaurus* is the world's largest freestanding dinosaur exhibit.

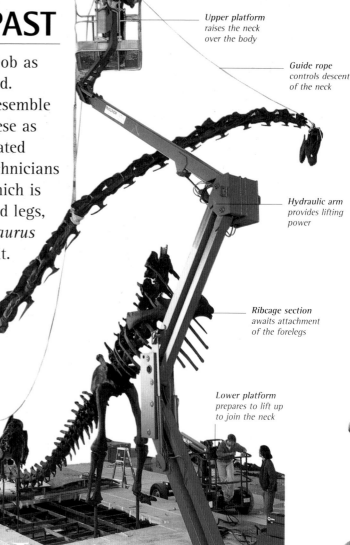

Upper platform raises the neck over the body

Guide rope controls descent of the neck

Hydraulic arm provides lifting power

Ribcage section awaits attachment of the forelegs

Lower platform prepares to lift up to join the neck

CREATING THE BAROSAURUS REPLICA

MAKING THE MOULDS
The fossilized bones were labelled with their positions within the skeleton. Each fossil bone was then thickly painted with liquid rubber. After it had set into a flexible mould of each fossil, the rubber was peeled away. Cotton gauze and plastic were added to the outside of each mould to strengthen it.

PREPARING FOR CASTING
The moulds of the long limb bones were made in two halves that fitted together exactly. The inside of each half was painted with a liquid plastic that would form the outer surface of the replica bone. The outsides of the moulds were stiffened with a fibreglass layer, and the halves were fitted together.

MAKING THE CAST
The hollow moulds with their inner linings of tough plastic were filled with another type of liquid plastic. This set in a rigid but honeycombed form, made lightweight by thousands of air bubbles. Without the strengthening of this solid foam-plastic core, the plastic inner linings might break.

REMOVING THE MOULD
Each mould was left until the foam-plastic casting inside had hardened. The mould with its tough outer jacket was then eased away to reveal the shape of the original fossil bone inside. The tough plastic outer surface of the cast was smoothed down and carefully painted to match the colouring of the fossil bone.

▲ ASSEMBLING THE SKELETON
With its head rearing more than 15 m (50 ft) into the air, the *Barosaurus* skeleton was mounted on a supporting metal frame. It took two hydraulic lifting platforms to assemble it safely. First the tail sections were joined together in their upward-curving shape. Then the tail's metal frame was welded to the frame of the hind legs. The huge ribcage followed. The assembled head and neck section was then raised above the body.

JOINING THE NECK ▶
The teams operating the two lifting platforms had to work very closely when the neck was ready to be fitted to the body. Suspended by strong ropes from the upper platform, the long neck section was inched downwards, with men on the ground pulling on ropes to help control its movement. A worker on the lower platform guided the neck's connecting rod until it finally slotted into a tube in the body's frame.

Lifting platform supports lower assembly team

Angle of neck
is adjusted as
it is lowered

▲ WELDING THE FRAMEWORK
Throughout the assembly process, welders
worked quickly to ensure that fitted sections
of the support frame could not come apart
again. Care was taken to shield the bones
from hot sparks, which could set them alight.
After a section of the frame was welded, part
of the replica skeleton was fitted over the
weld, hiding it from view.

Worker guides
the neck section
towards the body

Guide ropes stop
the neck from
swinging around

COMPLETED DISPLAY ▲
The awe-inspiring spectacle of the mother
Barosaurus protecting its young from a
ferocious *Allosaurus* greets visitors when they
first enter the museum. Scientists believe that
such a scene could have occurred 150 million
years ago, but it cannot be known for certain.
The replicas stand on a bare surface that, like
the dinosaur skeletons, was produced by a
moulding process. Latex rubber was painted
onto rocky ground in Montana; when the
rubber mould had set it was peeled away and
later used to make a cast of the rocky surface.

rebuilding

Ribcage is already
firmly welded to
the lower body

BIPEDAL CARNIVORES

The scientific name for meat-eating dinosaurs is theropods, which means "beast-footed". These fierce hunting carnivores were saurischian – they had hip bones arranged like those of a lizard. The pubis bone reached forward and down, the ischium bone reached down and back, and the ilium bone along the top held the leg muscles. Most of the carnivores were wholly bipedal, standing and running on their two back legs. Many, such as the efficient predators *Deinonychus* and *Suchomimus*, had long fingers and claws on their front legs, which they used to grip food or slash prey.

theropods

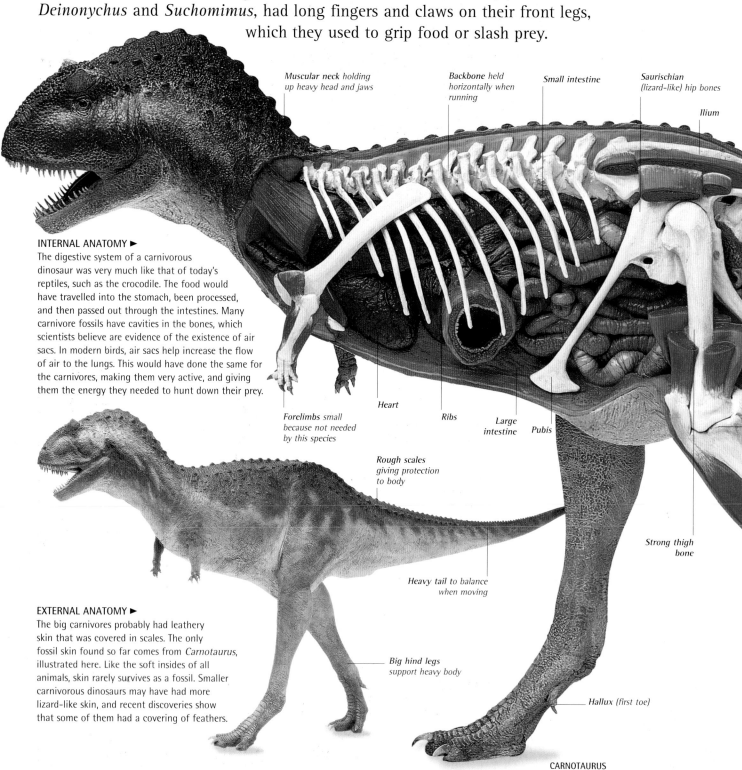

Muscular neck *holding up heavy head and jaws*

Backbone *held horizontally when running*

Small intestine

Saurischian *(lizard-like) hip bones*

Ilium

INTERNAL ANATOMY ▶
The digestive system of a carnivorous dinosaur was very much like that of today's reptiles, such as the crocodile. The food would have travelled into the stomach, been processed, and then passed out through the intestines. Many carnivore fossils have cavities in the bones, which scientists believe are evidence of the existence of air sacs. In modern birds, air sacs help increase the flow of air to the lungs. This would have done the same for the carnivores, making them very active, and giving them the energy they needed to hunt down their prey.

Forelimbs *small because not needed by this species*

Heart

Ribs

Large intestine

Pubis

Rough scales *giving protection to body*

Strong thigh bone

Heavy tail to balance *when moving*

EXTERNAL ANATOMY ▶
The big carnivores probably had leathery skin that was covered in scales. The only fossil skin found so far comes from *Carnotaurus*, illustrated here. Like the soft insides of all animals, skin rarely survives as a fossil. Smaller carnivorous dinosaurs may have had more lizard-like skin, and recent discoveries show that some of them had a covering of feathers.

Big hind legs *support heavy body*

Hallux *(first toe)*

CARNOTAURUS

SOME THEROPODS

TRIASSIC PERIOD

EORAPTOR

JURASSIC PERIOD

XUANHANOSAURUS

CERATOSAURUS

CRETACEOUS PERIOD

BARYONYX

SUCHOMIMUS

DEINONYCHUS

GALLIMIMUS

TYRANNOSAURUS

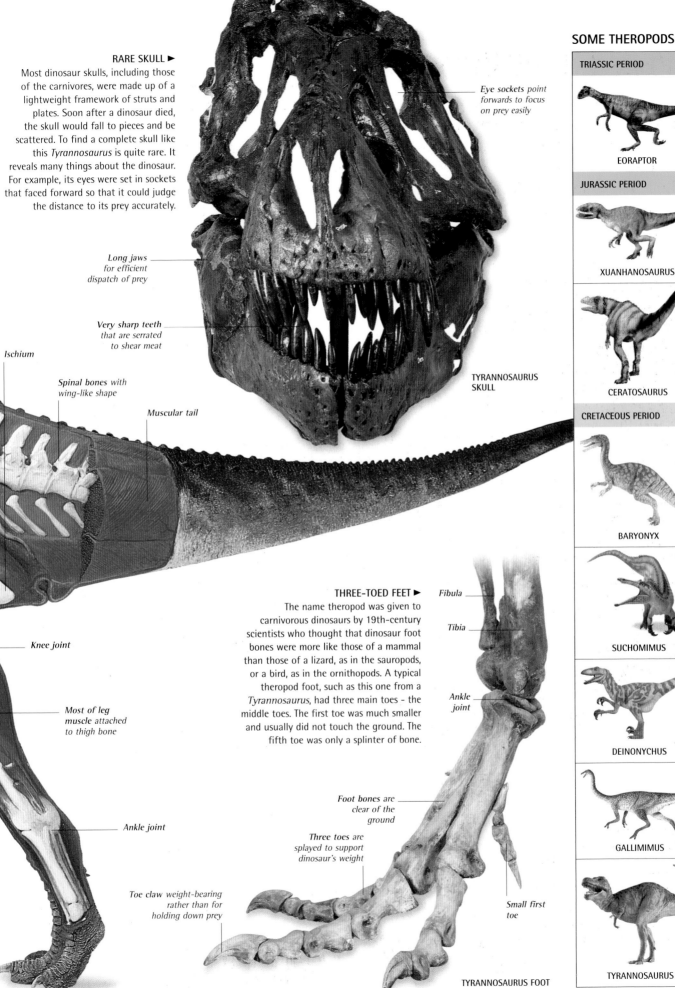

RARE SKULL ▶

Most dinosaur skulls, including those of the carnivores, were made up of a lightweight framework of struts and plates. Soon after a dinosaur died, the skull would fall to pieces and be scattered. To find a complete skull like this *Tyrannosaurus* is quite rare. It reveals many things about the dinosaur. For example, its eyes were set in sockets that faced forward so that it could judge the distance to its prey accurately.

Eye sockets point forwards to focus on prey easily

Long jaws for efficient dispatch of prey

Very sharp teeth that are serrated to shear meat

TYRANNOSAURUS SKULL

Ischium

Spinal bones with wing-like shape

Muscular tail

Knee joint

Most of leg muscle attached to thigh bone

Ankle joint

Toe claw weight-bearing rather than for holding down prey

THREE-TOED FEET ▶

The name theropod was given to carnivorous dinosaurs by 19th-century scientists who thought that dinosaur foot bones were more like those of a mammal than those of a lizard, as in the sauropods, or a bird, as in the ornithopods. A typical theropod foot, such as this one from a *Tyrannosaurus*, had three main toes - the middle toes. The first toe was much smaller and usually did not touch the ground. The fifth toe was only a splinter of bone.

Fibula

Tibia

Ankle joint

Foot bones are clear of the ground

Three toes are splayed to support dinosaur's weight

Small first toe

TYRANNOSAURUS FOOT

LONG-NECKED HERBIVORES

The biggest land animals to have lived on Earth were the sauropods, which means "lizard feet". These giants were the long-necked herbivorous (plant-eating) dinosaurs. They had small heads, long, flexible necks, bulky bodies, and long tails. They walked slowly on all fours and fed on conifers and other plants with tall stems. They existed for 130 million years, from the early Jurassic through to the late Cretaceous. Footprints show that they lived in herds or in family groups for protection against their cousins, the big carnivores.

Outer ear

Strong neck muscles

Eye

Snout

Strong tendon to support neck's weight

Long, flexible neck to reach tops of trees

Thick, scaly skin

EXTERNAL ANATOMY ►
The big digestive system of the long-necked herbivores had to be carried well forward of the lizard-like hips. This means that the animal could not have balanced on its hind legs only. Some of these dinosaurs, like this *Brachiosaurus*, had very long front legs, while others, such as *Apatosaurus*, did not. Their skin may have been elephant-like or possibly scaly. Some may also have had spines down their backs, for ornamentation and display.

Elephant-like feet

BRACHIOSAURUS

▼ INTERNAL ANATOMY
An animal that eats plants rather than meat needs a complex digestive system to break down the food. Long-necked herbivores such as this *Brachiosaurus* could not chew, so they swallowed plant food whole and it was ground up in their stomachs. They also swallowed gastroliths ("stomach stones"), which churned with the plants in the stomach, breaking them into smaller, more easily digestible pieces.

Oesophagus (gullet)

Big lungs

Shoulder joint

Heart

Gizzard holding gastroliths to break up plant food

Elbow joint

Leg bones are straight and vertical to carry heavy weight of body

BRACHIOSAURUS

PROSAUROPODS

The earliest long-necked herbivores were the prosauropods, which means "before lizard feet". Prosauropods evolved in the Late Triassic and died out in the Early Jurassic. They ranged from rabbit-sized lightweights that could scamper around on their hind legs, to lumbering elephant-sized animals that looked like the later sauropods. *Anchisaurus* was typical and about the size of a human being. It probably spent some of its time on its hind legs, but usually moved about on all fours. The earliest prosauropods were the ancestors of the sauropods.

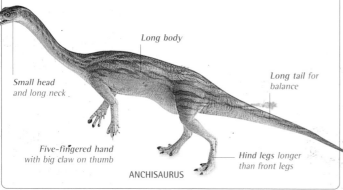

Long body

Small head and long neck

Long tail for balance

Five-fingered hand with big claw on thumb

Hind legs longer than front legs

ANCHISAURUS

▼ TEETH FOR RAKING

Sauropods fed by raking and swallowing – they did not chew. And they would have had to keep eating all the time to feed their great bodies. The teeth of a *Diplodocus* were peg-like and arranged like the teeth of a rake at the front of the jaw. The teeth of a *Camarasaurus* were more spoon-shaped and filled most of the jaw. Both were adapted for pulling food off trees.

Peg-like teeth

DIPLODOCUS SKULL

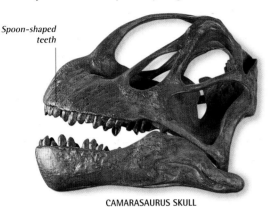

Spoon-shaped teeth

CAMARASAURUS SKULL

▲ TEETH FOR COMBING

The wear on the narrow teeth of *Diplodocus* fossils reveals a lot about how the dinosaur fed itself and what it ate. The angle the skull was held at, the length of the neck, and the different types of wear on the teeth show that *Diplodocus* probably fed in two ways. It could reach up and eat from the tops of the trees for some of the time, but it could also reach around it on or near the ground for low-growing plants.

PILLARLIKE LEGS ▶

Some sauropods weighed as much as 100 tonnes – about the same as a blue whale. Their legs had to be strong enough to support this weight. They walked on their tiptoes, but under the parts of the toes that were lifted from the ground there was a wedge of gristle. This spread out the weight and took the pressure off the toes themselves. Elephants have this kind of a foot for exactly the same reason.

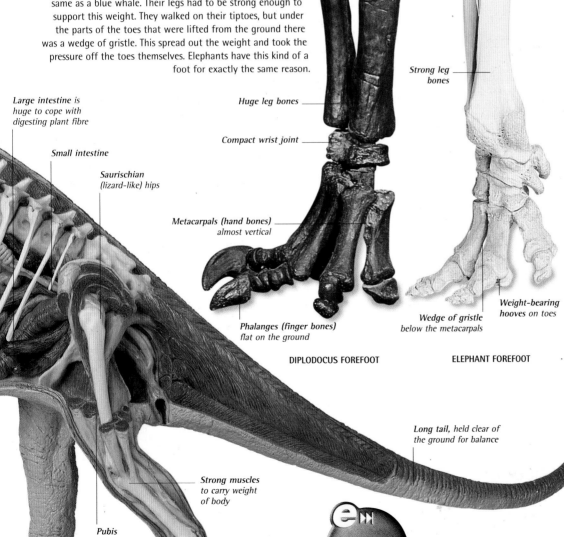

Large intestine is huge to cope with digesting plant fibre

Small intestine

Saurischian (lizard-like) hips

Huge leg bones

Compact wrist joint

Metacarpals (hand bones) almost vertical

Strong leg bones

Phalanges (finger bones) flat on the ground

DIPLODOCUS FOREFOOT

Wedge of gristle below the metacarpals

Weight-bearing hooves on toes

ELEPHANT FOREFOOT

Strong muscles to carry weight of body

Pubis

Ankle joint

Long tail, held clear of the ground for balance

e ▶▶
sauropods

SOME LONG-NECKED HERBIVORES

JURASSIC PERIOD

VULCANODON

BARAPASAURUS

BAROSAURUS

SEISMOSAURUS

CAMARASAURUS

CRETACEOUS PERIOD

TITANOSAURUS

SALTASAURUS

BIPEDAL HERBIVORES

As well as the giant plant-eaters, there were several other groups of smaller herbivores, including the ornithopods, which means "bird feet". These successful and widespread dinosaurs first appeared 200 million years ago in the Jurassic and were abundant in the Cretaceous. They had ornithischian (bird-like) hip bones and a big plant-eating gut carried well back. This allowed the animals to walk and run away from danger on their hind legs. Unlike the sauropods, their teeth and jaws were adapted for chewing plant material.

ornithopods

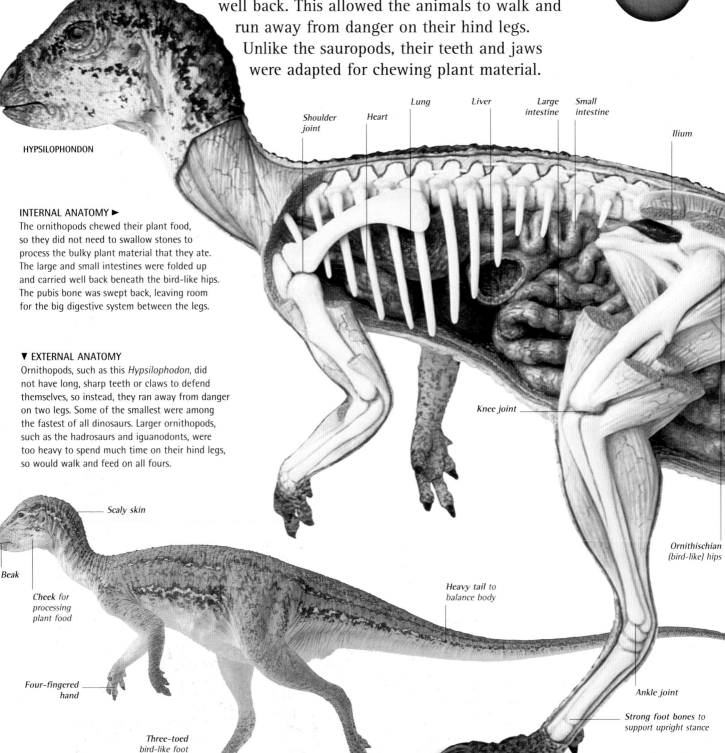

HYPSILOPHONDON

INTERNAL ANATOMY ▶
The ornithopods chewed their plant food, so they did not need to swallow stones to process the bulky plant material that they ate. The large and small intestines were folded up and carried well back beneath the bird-like hips. The pubis bone was swept back, leaving room for the big digestive system between the legs.

▼ EXTERNAL ANATOMY
Ornithopods, such as this *Hypsilophodon*, did not have long, sharp teeth or claws to defend themselves, so instead, they ran away from danger on two legs. Some of the smallest were among the fastest of all dinosaurs. Larger ornithopods, such as the hadrosaurs and iguanodonts, were too heavy to spend much time on their hind legs, so would walk and feed on all fours.

Shoulder joint

Heart

Lung

Liver

Large intestine

Small intestine

Ilium

Knee joint

Ornithischian (bird-like) hips

Scaly skin

Beak

Cheek for processing plant food

Four-fingered hand

Heavy tail to balance body

Ankle joint

Strong foot bones to support upright stance

Three-toed bird-like foot

HYPSILOPHODON

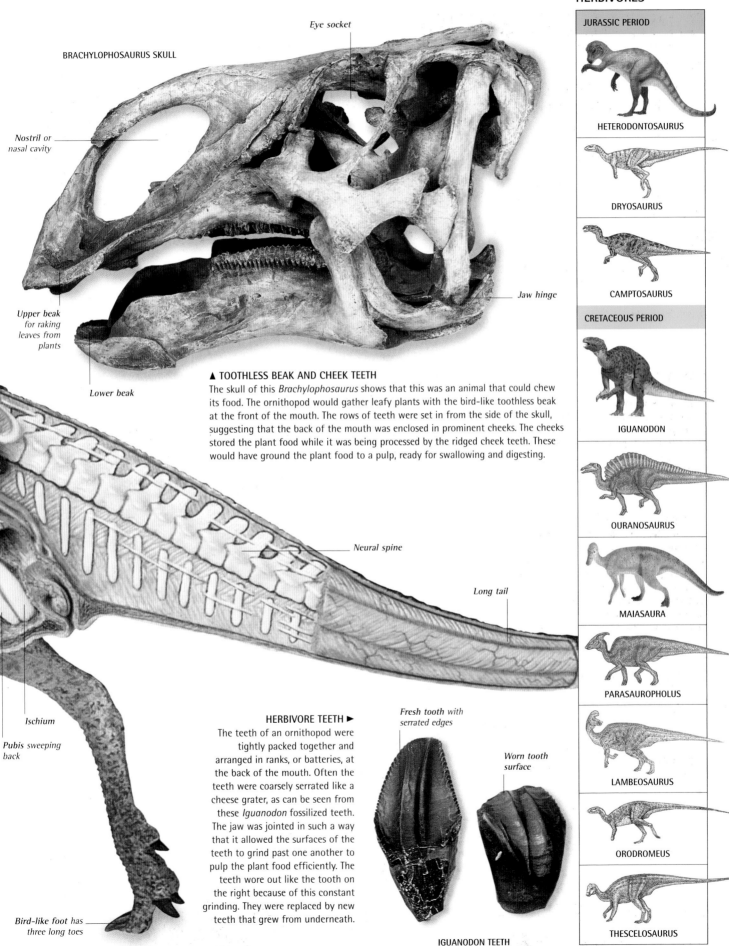

47

BRACHYLOPHOSAURUS SKULL

Eye socket

Nostril or
nasal cavity

Jaw hinge

Upper beak
for raking
leaves from
plants

Lower beak

▲ TOOTHLESS BEAK AND CHEEK TEETH

The skull of this *Brachylophosaurus* shows that this was an animal that could chew
its food. The ornithopod would gather leafy plants with the bird-like toothless beak
at the front of the mouth. The rows of teeth were set in from the side of the skull,
suggesting that the back of the mouth was enclosed in prominent cheeks. The cheeks
stored the plant food while it was being processed by the ridged cheek teeth. These
would have ground the plant food to a pulp, ready for swallowing and digesting.

Neural spine

Long tail

Ischium

Pubis sweeping
back

Bird-like foot has
three long toes

HERBIVORE TEETH ▶

The teeth of an ornithopod were
tightly packed together and
arranged in ranks, or batteries, at
the back of the mouth. Often the
teeth were coarsely serrated like a
cheese grater, as can be seen from
these *Iguanodon* fossilized teeth.
The jaw was jointed in such a way
that it allowed the surfaces of the
teeth to grind past one another to
pulp the plant food efficiently. The
teeth wore out like the tooth on
the right because of this constant
grinding. They were replaced by new
teeth that grew from underneath.

Fresh tooth with
serrated edges

Worn tooth
surface

IGUANODON TEETH

SOME BIPEDAL HERBIVORES

JURASSIC PERIOD

HETERODONTOSAURUS

DRYOSAURUS

CAMPTOSAURUS

CRETACEOUS PERIOD

IGUANODON

OURANOSAURUS

MAIASAURA

PARASAUROPHOLUS

LAMBEOSAURUS

ORODROMEUS

THESCELOSAURUS

HORNED AND ARMOURED

Three major groups of plant-eating dinosaurs were well equipped to defend themselves – some of the larger ones against the fiercest of the carnivores. The plated stegosaurs were largely a Jurassic group and were armed with plates and tail spines. The horned ceratopsians lived at the end of the Cretaceous and sported a heavy neck shield and an array of horns. The armoured ankylosaurs were among the last of the dinosaurs to appear and had backs covered with armoured shields and horny plates.

▼ EXTERNAL ANATOMY
The heavy horned, plated, or armoured dinosaurs walked on four feet. Their hind legs were bigger than the front legs, suggesting that the dinosaurs evolved from earlier two-footed types, possibly resembling ornithopods. Like the ornithopods, they had mouths adapted for chewing, with teeth that could chop or grind. They also had beaks at the front of their mouths and cheeks at the sides. Most carried a mosaic of fine studded armour, or flat plates called scutes, on their bodies.

Scaly skin covered with flat plates called scutes

Armoured body studded with spikes

Powerful legs to carry heavy body

Tail club could be wielded as a weapon

Toothless beak

EUOPLOCEPHALUS (AN ANKYLOSAUR)

Toes

Broad feet

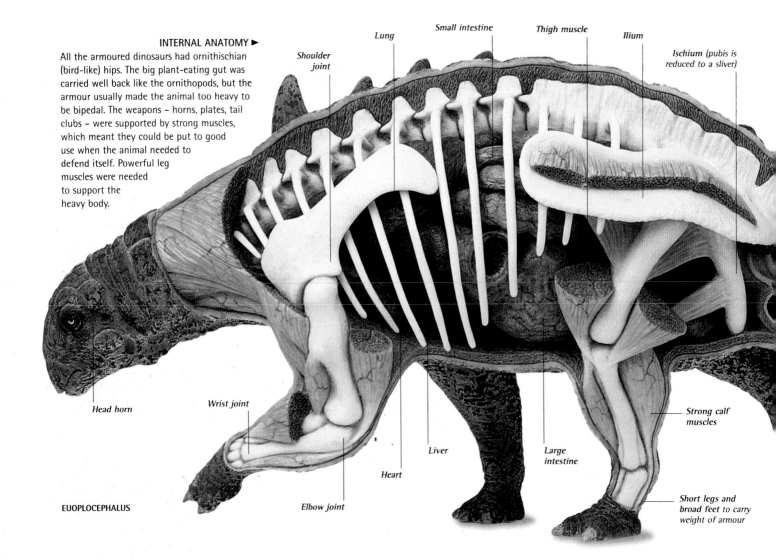

INTERNAL ANATOMY ▶
All the armoured dinosaurs had ornithischian (bird-like) hips. The big plant-eating gut was carried well back like the ornithopods, but the armour usually made the animal too heavy to be bipedal. The weapons – horns, plates, tail clubs – were supported by strong muscles, which meant they could be put to good use when the animal needed to defend itself. Powerful leg muscles were needed to support the heavy body.

Lung *Small intestine* *Thigh muscle* *Ilium*

Shoulder joint

Ischium (pubis is reduced to a sliver)

Head horn

Wrist joint

Strong calf muscles

EUOPLOCEPHALUS

Elbow joint

Heart

Liver

Large intestine

Short legs and broad feet to carry weight of armour

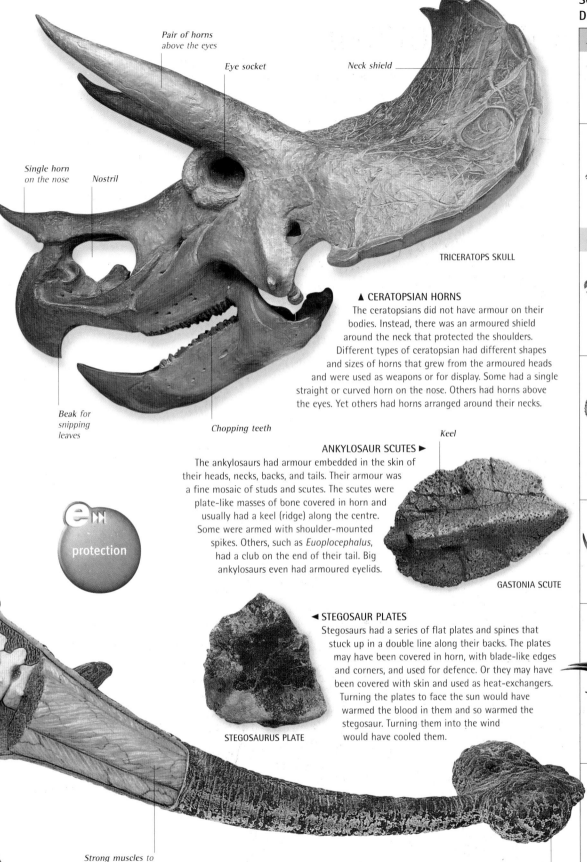

Pair of horns
above the eyes

Eye socket

Neck shield

Single horn
on the nose

Nostril

TRICERATOPS SKULL

Beak for
snipping
leaves

Chopping teeth

▲ CERATOPSIAN HORNS

The ceratopsians did not have armour on their
bodies. Instead, there was an armoured shield
around the neck that protected the shoulders.
Different types of ceratopsian had different shapes
and sizes of horns that grew from the armoured heads
and were used as weapons or for display. Some had a single
straight or curved horn on the nose. Others had horns above
the eyes. Yet others had horns arranged around their necks.

Keel

ANKYLOSAUR SCUTES ▶

The ankylosaurs had armour embedded in the skin of
their heads, necks, backs, and tails. Their armour was
a fine mosaic of studs and scutes. The scutes were
plate-like masses of bone covered in horn and
usually had a keel (ridge) along the centre.
Some were armed with shoulder-mounted
spikes. Others, such as *Euoplocephalus*,
had a club on the end of their tail. Big
ankylosaurs even had armoured eyelids.

protection

GASTONIA SCUTE

◀ STEGOSAUR PLATES

Stegosaurs had a series of flat plates and spines that
stuck up in a double line along their backs. The plates
may have been covered in horn, with blade-like edges
and corners, and used for defence. Or they may have
been covered with skin and used as heat-exchangers.
Turning the plates to face the sun would have
warmed the blood in them and so warmed the
stegosaur. Turning them into the wind
would have cooled them.

STEGOSAURUS PLATE

Strong muscles to
support heavy club
at end of tail

Thickened bone gave
tail its club shape

**SOME ARMOURED
DINOSAURS**

JURASSIC PERIOD

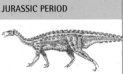

SCELIDOSAURUS

STEGOSAURUS

CRETACEOUS PERIOD

ACANTHOPHOLIS

PROTOCERATOPS

STYRACOSAURUS

PENTACERATOPS

ANKLYOSAURUS

TRICERATOPS

MOVING ABOUT

No-one has ever seen a dinosaur in action. However, the bones and the joints of fossilized skeletons can give us clues as to how the animals moved. Marks on the bones can show where the muscles were attached. The articulation of the bones (the way the bones move in relation to one another) shows how the limbs were flexed and how far they could reach. The size of the feet shows whether a dinosaur was a slow plodder (big, solid feet) or a fast runner (lightweight feet). Above all, scientists can find out more about dinosaurs by comparing what they know with the anatomy and lifestyle of modern animals.

▲ RUNNING STYLE OF AN OSTRICH
The modern equivalent of a running dinosaur would be one of today's flightless birds, such as an ostrich (above) or a rhea. Like a dinosaur, these keep their bodies horizontal and their heads high. The long legs, with their muscular thighs and their lightweight feet, are very similar to those of their theropod ancestors.

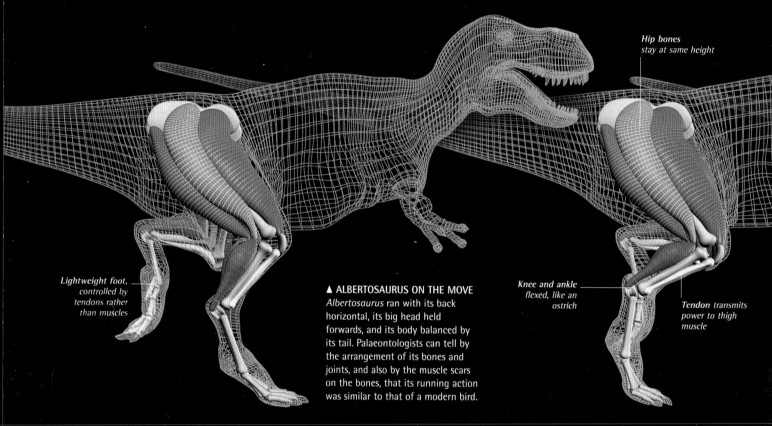

*Hip bones
stay at same height*

*Lightweight foot,
controlled by
tendons rather
than muscles*

▲ ALBERTOSAURUS ON THE MOVE
Albertosaurus ran with its back horizontal, its big head held forwards, and its body balanced by its tail. Palaeontologists can tell by the arrangement of its bones and joints, and also by the muscle scars on the bones, that its running action was similar to that of a modern bird.

*Knee and ankle
flexed, like an
ostrich*

*Tendon transmits
power to thigh
muscle*

HOW A TYRANNOSAURUS STOOD UP

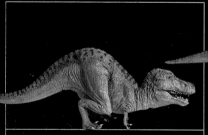

LEVERING UP
The shape of the hip bones suggests that *Tyrannosaurus* would have rested flat on its belly. While it was in this position, the weight of the hips would have been carried by the broad "boot" at the end of the pubis bone. How, then, did the dinosaur manage to stand up? It is possible that it used its tiny arms to give itself some leverage.

LEANING FORWARD
As *Tyrannosaurus* rose to its feet by straightening its legs, it would have been in danger of toppling forward and sliding along the ground. The little arms, however, would have gripped the ground and prevented this from happening. If the head was thrown backwards, this would have moved the centre of gravity back towards the hip.

UPRIGHT STANCE
The normal stance of a *Tyrannosaurus* was with the body held horizontally, the head pushed forwards, and the tail out at the back to provide balance. Like this, the dinosaur would have been a formidable fighting machine propelled by powerful legs, with its main weapons – its teeth – held well forward to attack or defend.

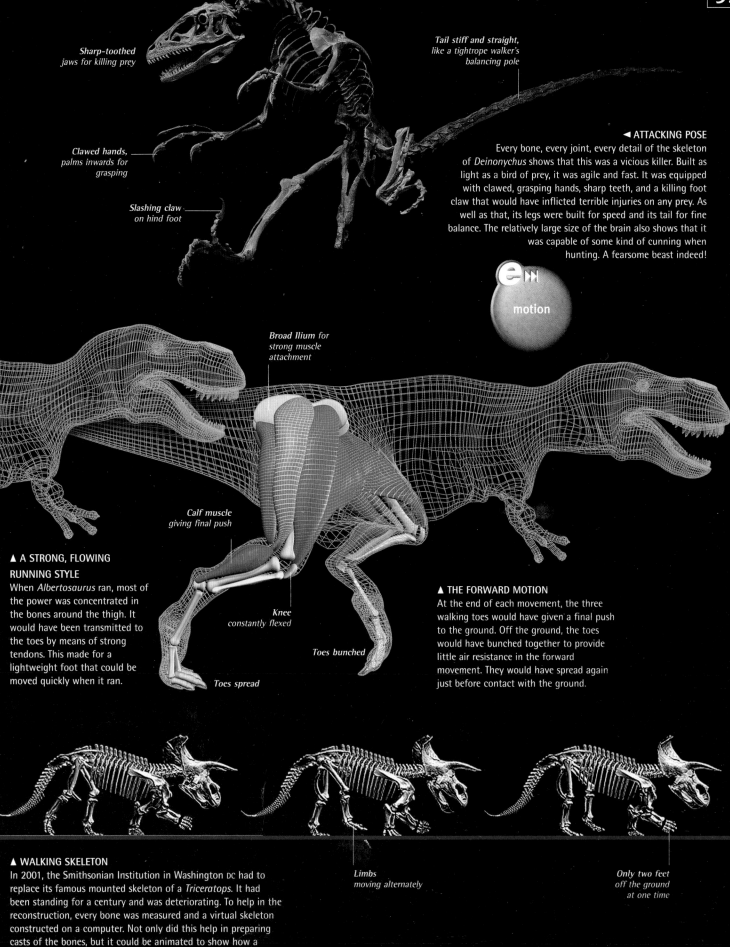

Sharp-toothed jaws for killing prey

Tail stiff and straight, like a tightrope walker's balancing pole

Clawed hands, palms inwards for grasping

Slashing claw on hind foot

◄ ATTACKING POSE

Every bone, every joint, every detail of the skeleton of *Deinonychus* shows that this was a vicious killer. Built as light as a bird of prey, it was agile and fast. It was equipped with clawed, grasping hands, sharp teeth, and a killing foot claw that would have inflicted terrible injuries on any prey. As well as that, its legs were built for speed and its tail for fine balance. The relatively large size of the brain also shows that it was capable of some kind of cunning when hunting. A fearsome beast indeed!

e ▸▸
motion

Broad Ilium for strong muscle attachment

Calf muscle giving final push

▲ A STRONG, FLOWING RUNNING STYLE

When *Albertosaurus* ran, most of the power was concentrated in the bones around the thigh. It would have been transmitted to the toes by means of strong tendons. This made for a lightweight foot that could be moved quickly when it ran.

Knee constantly flexed

Toes bunched

Toes spread

▲ THE FORWARD MOTION

At the end of each movement, the three walking toes would have given a final push to the ground. Off the ground, the toes would have bunched together to provide little air resistance in the forward movement. They would have spread again just before contact with the ground.

▲ WALKING SKELETON

In 2001, the Smithsonian Institution in Washington DC had to replace its famous mounted skeleton of a *Triceratops*. It had been standing for a century and was deteriorating. To help in the reconstruction, every bone was measured and a virtual skeleton constructed on a computer. Not only did this help in preparing casts of the bones, but it could be animated to show how a living *Triceratops* would have walked – how it swung its legs, how it carried its head and how it balanced with its tail.

Limbs moving alternately

Only two feet off the ground at one time

FEEDING

Throughout the dinosaur era, communities of dinosaurs were made up of plant-eaters (herbivores) and meat-eaters (carnivores). Different dinosaurs had different feeding habits. Giant herbivorous dinosaurs, such as the sauropods, munched high in the treetops. Smaller plant-eaters were well adapted for chomping on lower-level plants, or grazing on ground cover. Large predators, and medium-sized pack hunters, tended to eat the meat of other dinosaurs. Smaller meat-eaters ate animals such as lizards, and insects.

Special teeth inside the cheeks were used to grind food

◀ TREE-TOP BROWSER
Not only was the 40-tonne *Barosaurus* one of the heaviest sauropods of the Jurassic Period, it had one of the longest necks of any dinosaur. A fully grown adult measured about 27 m (89 ft) from nose to tail. Its neck accounted for one-third of its length. Why such a long neck? It is thought that *Barosaurus* stretched up to leaves that were out of reach of shorter-necked plant-eaters.

Long tail may have been used as a prop

Barosaurus's centre of gravity was near the hips

▲ BALANCING ACT
Barosaurus had short front legs and longer back legs. This meant there was less weight at the front its body, so it may have been able to rock back on its hind legs, lifting its lightweight front legs off the ground to reach up to plants growing 15 m (49 ft) above the ground. It could have used its tail to support it in this stretching position. *Barosaurus* could not have remained upright for very long as its bones and muscles would have been under considerable strain.

Long neck was supported by stretched tendons

Front limbs were short compared to hind limbs

Triceratops's **beak** was worn down by its rough diet, but continued to grow during its lifetime

▲ LOW BROWSER

Triceratops lived about 70 million years ago, at the end of the Cretaceous Period. It ate the new flowering plants that first appeared at this time, such as magnolia, oak, and laurel. *Triceratops* used its sharp beak to snip off leaves, twigs, and bark, and could reach food that grew up to 3 m (9 ft) from the ground. Only taller plants were safe from its giant appetite. It lived in herds, and grazed in forests and along the edges of rivers and swamps.

VEGETARIAN MOUTHS

DIFFERENT-TOOTHED MOUTH
Heterodontosaurus had three kinds of teeth. Incisors at the front of the top jaw were used for cutting. Tusk-like teeth may have been used for defence. Chisel-like teeth were for shredding food plants.

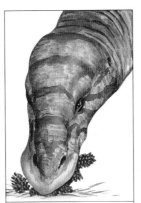

MIXED DIET
Edmontosaurus had a broad snout for gathering up big mouthfuls of different kinds of vegetation. It used its toothless beak for cropping, and its cheek teeth for cutting up and chewing food.

PICKY EATER
Hypsilophodon had high-ridged cheek teeth, which made it very efficient at chewing tough vegetation. Its narrow mouth helped this dinosaur to choose which plants to pick at.

Tail was held above the ground when the animal was on all fours

feeding

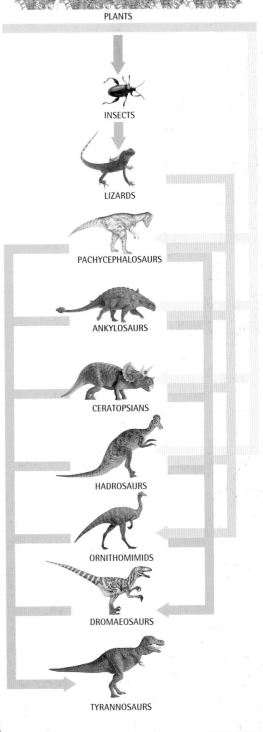

CRETACEOUS FOOD CHAIN

Any animal community has food chains of predators and prey. Interlinked chains form a food web. This diagram shows who ate whom in Late Cretaceous western North America. Arrows point to the predator. The top predators were the tyrannosaurs, but all dinosaurs ultimately depended on plants.

FOOD CHAIN KEY
- Insect food
- Lizard food
- Herbivores' food
- Ornithomimid food
- Dromaeosaur food
- Tyrannosaur food

PLANTS
INSECTS
LIZARDS
PACHYCEPHALOSAURS
ANKYLOSAURS
CERATOPSIANS
HADROSAURS
ORNITHOMIMIDS
DROMAEOSAURS
TYRANNOSAURS

DIGESTIVE SYSTEMS

Carnivorous and herbivorous dinosaurs are quite easy to tell apart. As well as the different types of jaws and teeth, their body shapes were distinct from one another because of the different digestive systems they needed to absorb their food. Carnivores had much simpler digestive systems than herbivores, and their hip bones were arranged differently. These two characteristics meant that the carnivorous theropods were two-legged, the herbivorous sauropods were four-legged, and the herbivorous ornithopods could move around on either their hind legs or on all fours.

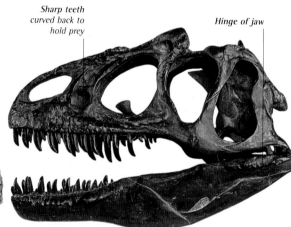

Thin blade-like body of tooth

Fine serrations along the cutting edge

▲ CARNIVORE'S SERRATED TOOTH

The tooth of a carnivorous dinosaur such as *Tyrannosaurus* is shaped like a steak knife. It is narrow like a blade, for slicing through flesh. It is also pointed for making incisions in its prey. Its edges had dozens of little serrations, like a fine saw, to tear through tough meat and tendons. Carnivore teeth quickly wore out and were easily damaged, breaking off if the dinosaur chomped on bone. Inside a carnivore's jaw, other teeth were constantly growing and replacing those teeth that were lost.

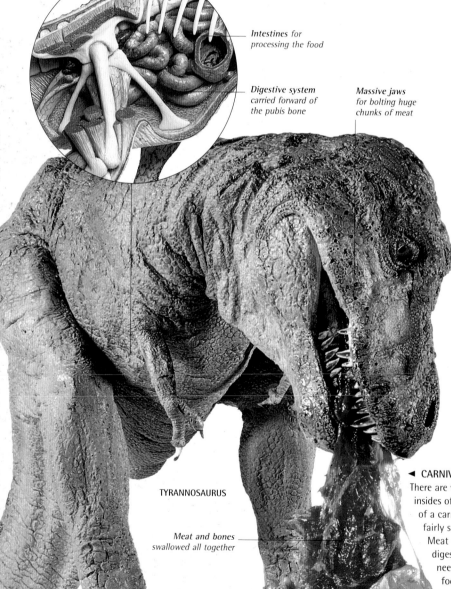

Intestines for processing the food

Digestive system carried forward of the pubis bone

Massive jaws for bolting huge chunks of meat

Sharp teeth curved back to hold prey

Hinge of jaw

TYRANNOSAURUS

Meat and bones swallowed all together

CARNIVORE'S JAWS FOR TEARING ▲

A carnivore's skull, like this one of an *Allosaurus*, was arranged so that it could work backwards and forwards. This movement allowed the rows of teeth to shear past each other, tearing the flesh of its prey between them. The teeth were curved back like barbs, so that anything held in its jaws would not stuggle out. The lightweight latticework of the skull and jaws meant that the sides of the mouth were able to move outwards. This widened the mouth so that the carnivore could swallow huge mouthfuls.

◄ CARNIVORE'S STOMACH

There are very few fossils that actually show the insides of a dinosaur. However, the digestive system of a carnivore would have been quite simple and fairly small compared with the size of the animal. Meat does not have tough fibres, so it is easily digested, and a carnivorous dinosaur did not need the huge guts of a herbivore to process its food. Nearly all of the carnivore's digestive system would have been carried in front of the pubis bone of the lizard-like hips. This compact arrangement would have allowed the dinosaur to move swiftly when chasing its prey.

feeding

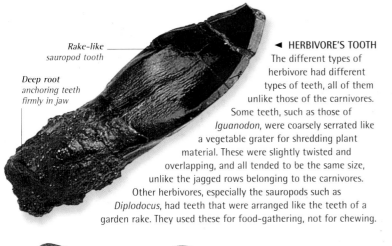

Rake-like
sauropod tooth

Deep root
anchoring teeth
firmly in jaw

◀ HERBIVORE'S TOOTH

The different types of herbivore had different types of teeth, all of them unlike those of the carnivores. Some teeth, such as those of *Iguanodon*, were coarsely serrated like a vegetable grater for shredding plant material. These were slightly twisted and overlapping, and all tended to be the same size, unlike the jagged rows belonging to the carnivores. Other herbivores, especially the sauropods such as *Diplodocus*, had teeth that were arranged like the teeth of a garden rake. They used these for food-gathering, not for chewing.

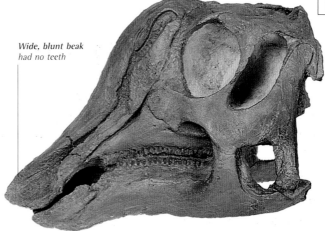

Wide, blunt beak
had no teeth

HERBIVORE'S JAWS FOR GRINDING ▲

This skull of a young *Lambeosaurus* shows the features of a typical ornithopod. The front of the mouth has a beak for snipping shoots and gathering plants. The position of the teeth right inside the mouth shows that there were cheek pouches at the side. The teeth were arranged in grinding rows or batteries that slid past each other, pulping the food while it was held in the cheeks. The angle of the jaw hinge helped the chewing muscles to work efficiently.

Surface worn smooth
by grinding together

Efficient grinding
teeth

Cheeks held the plant
food while chewing

Shorter neck
than a sauropod

▲ STOMACH STONES

Sauropods spent all their time raking the leaves from trees and plants and swallowing them. They did not chew because their teeth were the wrong shape. So, to break down their food, the herbivores swallowed stones. These gathered in an area of the stomach called the gizzard, forming a grinding mill to mash up the plant material. Skeletons of sauropods are sometimes found with polished stones, or gastroliths. Today's plant-eating birds, such as chickens, swallow grit for the same reason.

FEATURES OF A SAUROPOD'S STOMACH

The digestive system of a sauropod such as this *Brachiosaurus* was much bigger than that of the carnivores. It needed a large gut to break down the fibres in the plant material it ate. A sauropod would also have had a gizzard, where stomach stones ground up the food before it was passed into the stomach. All this weight had to be carried in front of the pubis bone, and that is why most sauropods could not support themselves for long on just their back legs.

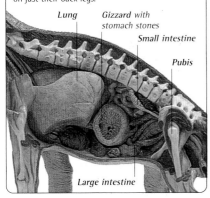

Lung

Gizzard with
stomach stones

Small intestine

Pubis

Large intestine

▲ ORNITHOPOD'S STOMACH

The digestive system of a two-footed ornithopod was much bigger than that of a carnivore – more like a sauropod's. However, unlike in a sauropod, it was carried well back in the body and the pubis bone was swept back out of the way. This meant the centre of gravity of the animal was much nearer the hips and it could move about on its hind legs. It also lacked a gizzard. With its efficient chewing system, an ornithopod did not need stomach stones.

IGUANODON

ATTACK

Flesh-eating dinosaurs had different methods of attack that varied with their size, agility, and victims. Large predators crept up on giant herbivores and killed them with a sudden charge. Smaller hunters chased game at speed. Predators struck mainly with their fangs and claws, but some, such as *Baryonyx*, might have seized fish in their crocodile-like jaws. It is also possible that certain dinosaurs poisoned their unfortunate victims with a toxic bite.

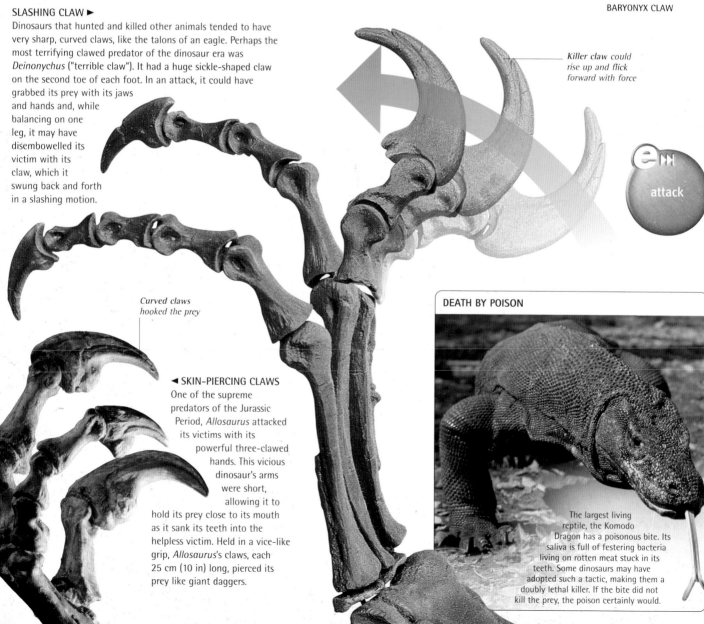

▲ SNATCH AND GRAB
Standing perfectly still, knee-high in water, *Baryonyx* might have snatched up unsuspecting fish in its narrow jaws, and pierced the scaly prey with its slender teeth. It may also have used its powerful forelimbs and curved thumb claws to hook fish from the water. We know this dinosaur ate fish because palaeontologists found the scales of *Lepidotes*, a large fish, in its ribcage.

BARYONYX CLAW

SLASHING CLAW ▶
Dinosaurs that hunted and killed other animals tended to have very sharp, curved claws, like the talons of an eagle. Perhaps the most terrifying clawed predator of the dinosaur era was *Deinonychus* ("terrible claw"). It had a huge sickle-shaped claw on the second toe of each foot. In an attack, it could have grabbed its prey with its jaws and hands and, while balancing on one leg, it may have disembowelled its victim with its claw, which it swung back and forth in a slashing motion.

Killer claw could rise up and flick forward with force

attack

Curved claws hooked the prey

◀ SKIN-PIERCING CLAWS
One of the supreme predators of the Jurassic Period, *Allosaurus* attacked its victims with its powerful three-clawed hands. This vicious dinosaur's arms were short, allowing it to hold its prey close to its mouth as it sank its teeth into the helpless victim. Held in a vice-like grip, *Allosaurus*'s claws, each 25 cm (10 in) long, pierced its prey like giant daggers.

DEATH BY POISON

The largest living reptile, the Komodo Dragon has a poisonous bite. Its saliva is full of festering bacteria living on rotten meat stuck in its teeth. Some dinosaurs may have adopted such a tactic, making them a doubly lethal killer. If the bite did not kill the prey, the poison certainly would.

CHASING DOWN PREY ▶

Compsognathus and other lightweight theropods had a slender build, with long necks and balancing tails. Such features would have made them fast sprinters. These predators would have used their speed and agility to pursue lizards, frogs, and other small creatures. When they caught up with them, they either grabbed them with their clawed hands, or thrust out their long necks and snapped up their victim with their narrow, sharp-toothed jaws.

Jaws agape and ready to snap shut on a victim

SUDDEN AMBUSH ▶

Giganotosaurus was an immense carnivore. It probably hunted by ambush, hiding in trees until a slow-moving herbivore came by. With jaws gaping wide, *Giganotosaurus* could have run at its prey head on. Powerful muscles slammed its jaw shut, and its 18 cm- (7 in-) long teeth sliced deep into its victim's flesh. Like a tiger, it probably gorged itself, then went days before its next meal.

Bony tail was held
stiff and straight
as Gallimimus ran

Three, clawed toes
on each foot

▲ SPRINT FROM DANGER
Not all dinosaurs were huge and lumbering.
Some were built for speed, which they used
to beat a hasty retreat from attackers.
Gallimimus had the physical features of
a sprinter. With its long, thin back legs,
Gallimimus could take large strides
efficiently, and its light body was perfectly
balanced by a slender tail. By measuring
their legs and comparing their shape to
those of modern animals, experts have
estimated that *Gallimimus* reached speeds
of 56 kph (35 mph). This is almost as fast
as a racehorse, and certainly speedy enough
to evade capture by a larger predator, such
as *Tyrannosaurus*.

DEFENCE

The dinosaur world was not over-run by gangs of vicious killers.
Most dinosaurs were peaceful creatures that never attacked
anything. Even so, each group had different ways of protecting
itself against attack. For speedy dinosaurs, being able to out-run
a predator was their main means of self-defence. Large sauropods
may have used their great bulk to intimidate their enemies.
Some dinosaurs carried weapons to defend themselves, striking
back with their tails, horns, or claws. Other dinosaurs
were more passive and relied on camouflage or body
armour for their protection.

protection

◄ BLENDING IN
Well-preserved fossils of dinosaur
skin are rare and do not show
the colour of the skin. We
know that patterns and colour
help modern reptiles to hide
from their enemies, so it
seems certain dinosaurs
would also have used colour
to blend in with their
surroundings. If *Iguanodon*
was green, it might have
escaped detection by the
flesh-eating predators that
prowled its forest home.

Long, flexible
neck helped
with balance

CLUB TAIL ▶

No living reptiles have defensive tails with attachments
as spectacular as the clubs used by the ankylosaurs. The
huge club at the end of *Euoplocephalus's* tail was made
out of several chunks of bone, all fused together into a
single lump. Powerful tail muscles were used
to swing the tail from side to side, delivering
a bone-shattering blow to an attacker.

EUOPLOCEPHALUS TAIL

Tail club weighed
up to 2 kg (4½ lb)

Tail was about
14 m (45 ft) long

DIPLODOCUS TAIL

◀ WHIP TAIL

Heavy and lumbering sauropods, such as *Diplodocus*,
could inflict stinging blows on attackers with their tapered,
whip-like tails. Apart from their daunting size, this was their main form of
defence. The ends of their tails were made up of narrow, cyclinder-shaped
bones which were designed to lash out sharply. The mere sound of
the tail cracking may have scared away a predator.

ARMOURED JACKET ▼

With their protective studs, plates, and spikes, armoured dinosaurs
were like walking fortresses. When under attack, they may have
crouched down to protect their soft bellies, presenting a
completely armoured shell. The armoured dinosaurs evolved
from small, lightweight species with just a few rows of studs
on their back into huge beasts with full suits of armour.

GASTONIA
ARMOUR

Spikes and
studs were fixed
to the skin, not
the skeleton

WINNING A MATE

All animals must reproduce themselves if their species is to survive. Today's animals have developed their own special ways of attracting mates. They send out signals through displays of body colour and distinctive call signs, and also by behaving differently at certain times of the year. By observing modern animals, it is possible to suggest how dinosaurs might have found their mates. Some species of dinosaurs developed highly distinctive features, such as head crests, bone skull domes, and extra-long face horns. Each of these features may have had its own uses in helping its owner to win a mate.

HEAD BANGERS ▶

The thick, domed skulls of *Pachycephalosaurus* earned them the name "bone-headed dinosaurs". With their brains protected by the bone, rival males may have head-butted each other when fighting over females – much like goats and sheep do today. Features of *Pachycephalosaurus's* vertebrae suggest that its spine may have been able to absorb a considerable amount of shock, so they may also have butted each other's bodies during a fight.

PENTACERATOPS SKULL

Brow horns grew above its eyes

▼ BATTLING MALES

In a Late Cretaceous woodland clearing in North America, about 70 million years ago, a pair of adult *Pentaceratops* face up to each other in a contest for a mate. Their neck frills are covered in richly patterned skin, perhaps designed to impress females. The bone frills also act like shields, deflecting stabs from incoming horns and protecting the animals' soft bodies. At the end of the battle, the winner celebrates by snorting triumphantly and pawing at the ground.

◀ FIVE-HORNED FACE WITH FRILLS

Pentaceratops means "five-horned face", but despite it name, this dinosaur really had three horns. It had a pair of long, curved ones on its forehead and a short horn on its snout. The other two "horns" that seemed to grow from the sides of its face were actually extended cheek bones. *Pentaceratops's* fantastic frill was nearly 1 m (3 ft) wide. Huge, empty, skin-covered gaps in the bone meant the frill was lightweight.

Opponent
shoves rival to
gain ground

Hard head
could withstand very
heavy knocks

mating

BIGGEST BONE-HEAD ▶

Pachycephalosaurus had the largest skull of all
the bone-headed dinosaurs. Its head was 80 cm
(2 ft 7 in) long and the dome was made of solid
bone 25 cm (10 in) thick. There were bony
nodules at the back, and on its snout were
several short, bony spikes. These would
have scratched and scraped an opponent
in a head-to-head tussle.

PACHYCEPHALOSAURUS
SKULL

HEAD CREST FOR COURTING

Corythosaurus was a member of the hadrosaur, or
duck-bill, family of dinosaurs. On top of its head
was a semi-circular, helmet-shaped bony crest.
Males appear to have grown larger crests than
females. This suggests they may have been used
in courtship rituals when males competed for the
attention of females. The crests may have been
coloured, perhaps changing colour in the mating
season. Inside the crests were passages, through
which *Corythosaurus* could snort and blow to
make distinctive sounds. These sounds could have
been mating calls which attracted the females.

*Skin on crest
may have had an
eye-catching pattern*

CORYTHOSAURUS

◀ RUTTING STAGS

Ideas of how the horned
dinosaurs used their frills and
horns come partly from the
rutting behaviour of modern
stags (male deer). In autumn,
the rutting season takes place,
when adult stags compete
for hinds (females). Stags
roar at each other, then clash
heads and lock antlers in an
attempt to shove each other
backwards. The one who gains
the most ground gets to mate
with the hinds.

BODY TEMPERATURE

Scientists cannot agree whether dinosaurs were cold-blooded or warm-blooded. Cold-blooded animals, such as reptiles, become hot or cold, depending on the temperature of their environment. Warm-blooded animals, such as birds, have a regulation system that keeps the body temperature constant. A warm-blooded animal needs to eat ten times as much food as a cold-blooded animal, just to fuel this system. It seems likely that giant herbivores, such as sauropods, could not have eaten enough to support such a system, and were cold-blooded. The carnivorous, active theropods, however, may have been warm-blooded.

When too cold a lizard warms up by basking in the heat of the sun

When too hot a lizard hides in the shade

▲ TEMPERATURE CONTROL
A lizard shows the behaviour typical of a cold-blooded animal. It has no internal mechanism to regulate its body temperature. When the environment turns cold, the lizard becomes cold and inactive. When the environment heats up, the lizard warms up too, and becomes active. It is capable of great bursts of speed, but it has to spend much of its time either basking in the sun or hiding in the shade.

SOLAR PANELS ▼
Stegosaurus was one of the plated dinosaurs, with a series of bony plates up along its back. When it was discovered, in the 1870s, scientists assumed the plates were covered in horn and used for defence. Then, a century later, tracks of blood vessels were found in fossils of the plates. This gave rise to the idea that the plates may actually have been covered in skin, not horn, and used for temperature regulation instead of defence.

temperature

Blood vessels control temperature by distributing heat around the body, or removing excess heat to cool the body

Blood-rich skin would have covered the plates if they worked as heat-exchangers

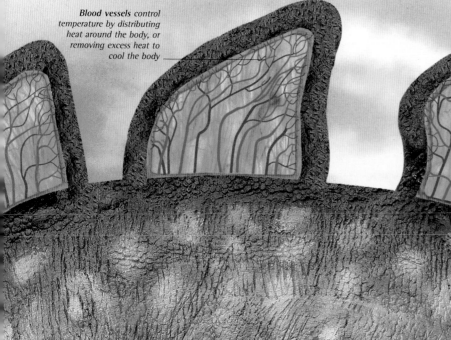

FUZZY RAPTOR

The fine detail of the feathers is preserved in volcanic dust

Soft, downy feathers on the body would have been used for insulation

Each hand had 3 long, narrow fingers with sharp claws

ENLARGED VIEW OF FEATHER-COVERED BODY

For decades scientists have argued over whether dinosaurs were warm-blooded or cold-blooded. Proof was hard to find, one way or another. Then, at the turn of this century, the beautifully preserved fossil of a chicken-sized theropod was found in China. The detailed fossil showed that the animal was covered in fine feathers. Only warm-blooded animals would need an insulating covering such as this. For many scientists, the discovery was the evidence they had been looking for. It showed that the small theropods, at least, were warm-blooded and had an active lifestyle. As yet, this feathered dromaeosaur has not been given a scientific name, and is only referred to as the "fuzzy raptor". The discovery of this fossil also seems to support the theory that birds evolved from meat-eating dinosaurs.

Tail feathers would have been used for display

COMPLETE SKELETON OF A FUZZY RAPTOR

HEAT REGULATION ▶

If the plates of *Stegosaurus* were used for temperature regulation, they might have worked a little like solar panels. If the animal was feeling cold, it could turn so that the broad sides of its plates, with their large surface area, faced the sun to absorb its heat. If it wanted to cool down, the animal would turn its plates away from the sun. It might also turn to find a position in the wind so moving air would circulate around the plates and cool them.

Plates may also have served to attract mates, or to help animals of the same species to recognize each other

Circulation of air around the plates would carry excess heat away

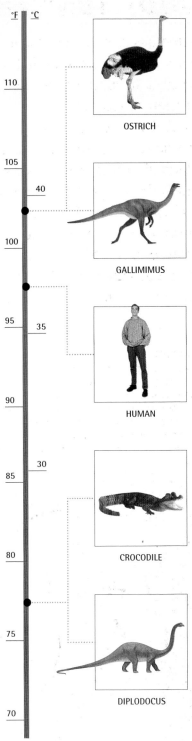

OSTRICH

GALLIMIMUS

HUMAN

CROCODILE

DIPLODOCUS

▲ IDEAL BODY TEMPERATURE
Different animals function best at different body temperatures. Active, warm-blooded animals tend to have higher ideal body temperatures than slow, cold-blooded types. The ideal body temperature varies between animal types, with warm-blooded and cold-blooded animals at either end of a gradual scale. It may be that dinosaurs ranged along a similar scale, with big plant-eaters, like sauropod's functioning rather like cold-blooded reptiles, and active theropods at the higher end of the scale, with birds. Other dinosaurs may have ranged between these two extremes.

BRAINS AND INTELLIGENCE

intelligence

How intelligent were dinosaurs? It is difficult to know how smart dinosaurs were because their brains rarely survive as fossils. Casts taken from the inside of fossil skulls show that some dinosaurs had large brains, while others had small ones. A big brain does not necessarily mean higher intelligence. Scientists look at the size of the brain in relation to the animal's total body weight. They also take into account the animal's behaviour. A dinosaur's intelligence was suited to its lifestyle and the tasks it needed to perform.

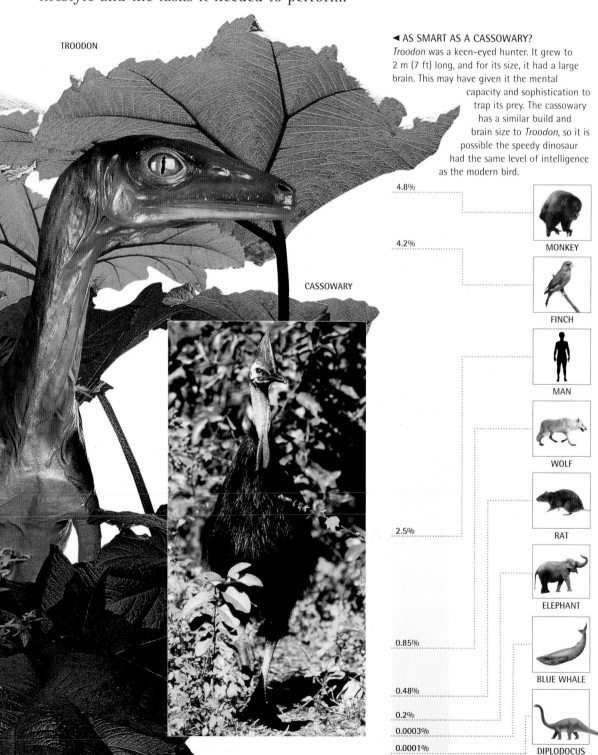

TROODON

CASSOWARY

◄ AS SMART AS A CASSOWARY?
Troodon was a keen-eyed hunter. It grew to 2 m (7 ft) long, and for its size, it had a large brain. This may have given it the mental capacity and sophistication to trap its prey. The cassowary has a similar build and brain size to *Troodon*, so it is possible the speedy dinosaur had the same level of intelligence as the modern bird.

4.8% — MONKEY

4.2% — FINCH

MAN

WOLF

2.5% — RAT

ELEPHANT

0.85% — BLUE WHALE

0.48%

0.2%

0.0003%

0.0001% — DIPLODOCUS

◄ BRAIN TO BODY WEIGHT
This diagram shows the weight of an animal's brain as a percentage of the weight of its body. Dinosaurs had smaller brains relative to their size than birds or mammals. At the bottom of the chart, *Diplodocus* had a brain weighing 100,000 times less than its body weight. Compare this with a small bird's brain, which is only 12 times lighter than its overall weight. The brain of an adult human is about 40 times lighter than its body. This is about the same ratio as the brain to body weight of a mouse. These comparisons alone should not be used to indicate intelligence, which must also be judged on how animals behave in comparison with other animals in their environment.

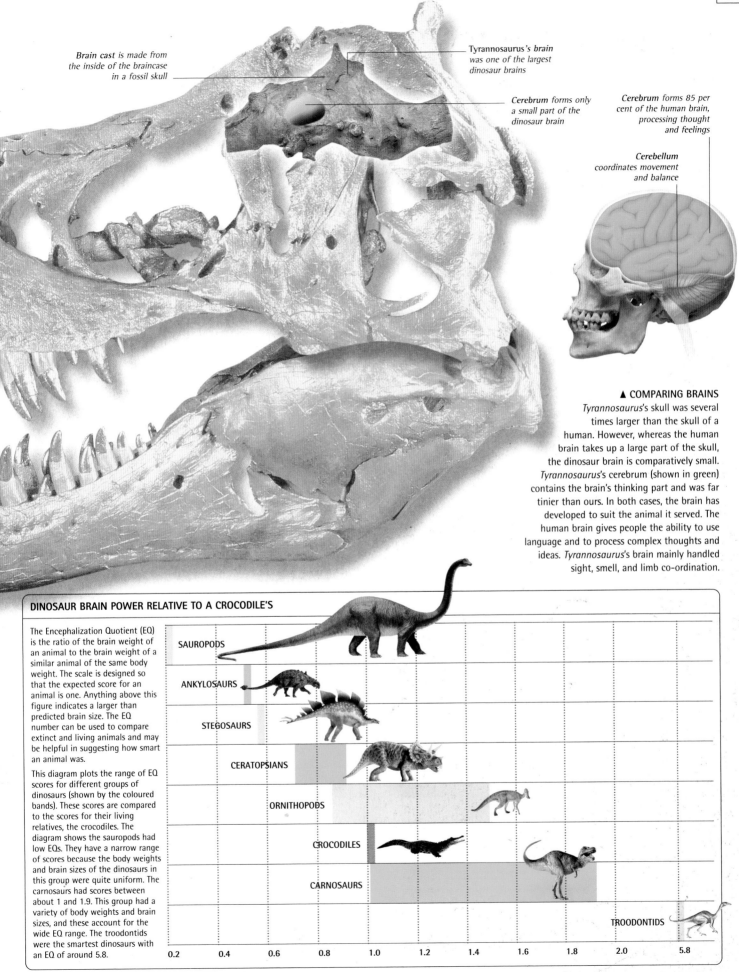

Brain cast is made from the inside of the braincase in a fossil skull

Tyrannosaurus's brain was one of the largest dinosaur brains

Cerebrum forms only a small part of the dinosaur brain

Cerebrum forms 85 per cent of the human brain, processing thought and feelings

Cerebellum coordinates movement and balance

▲ COMPARING BRAINS

Tyrannosaurus's skull was several times larger than the skull of a human. However, whereas the human brain takes up a large part of the skull, the dinosaur brain is comparatively small. *Tyrannosaurus's* cerebrum (shown in green) contains the brain's thinking part and was far tinier than ours. In both cases, the brain has developed to suit the animal it served. The human brain gives people the ability to use language and to process complex thoughts and ideas. *Tyrannosaurus's* brain mainly handled sight, smell, and limb co-ordination.

DINOSAUR BRAIN POWER RELATIVE TO A CROCODILE'S

The Encephalization Quotient (EQ) is the ratio of the brain weight of an animal to the brain weight of a similar animal of the same body weight. The scale is designed so that the expected score for an animal is one. Anything above this figure indicates a larger than predicted brain size. The EQ number can be used to compare extinct and living animals and may be helpful in suggesting how smart an animal was.

This diagram plots the range of EQ scores for different groups of dinosaurs (shown by the coloured bands). These scores are compared to the scores for their living relatives, the crocodiles. The diagram shows the sauropods had low EQs. They have a narrow range of scores because the body weights and brain sizes of the dinosaurs in this group were quite uniform. The carnosaurs had scores between about 1 and 1.9. This group had a variety of body weights and brain sizes, and these account for the wide EQ range. The troodontids were the smartest dinosaurs with an EQ of around 5.8.

SAUROPODS

ANKYLOSAURS

STEGOSAURS

CERATOPSIANS

ORNITHOPODS

CROCODILES

CARNOSAURS

TROODONTIDS

| 0.2 | 0.4 | 0.6 | 0.8 | 1.0 | 1.2 | 1.4 | 1.6 | 1.8 | 2.0 | 5.8 |

SENSES

Perhaps the most difficult part of dinosaurs' make-up to study is their senses. Were they slow and stupid, or were they alert and intelligent? Delicate organs such as brains and nerves do not fossilize well, and the bones associated with the sense organs are difficult to interpret. For example, it is impossible to find out about a dinosaur's senses of taste or smell – structures in the nasal cavities may be to do with either smelling or breathing. However, it is possible to make educated guesses about how a dinosaur sensory system would have worked.

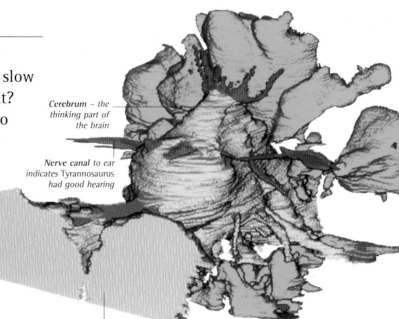

Cerebrum – the thinking part of the brain

Nerve canal to ear indicates Tyrannosaurus had good hearing

Larger olfactory bulbs show dinosaur had a good sense of smell

▲ 3-D MODEL OF A TYRANNOSAURUS BRAIN

Brains do not fossilize, but the bones that surround them do. Sometimes it is possible to tell the shape of a dinosaur's brain by looking at the gap left between the bones. If a skull has escaped being crushed, electronic scanning can produce a three-dimensional image of the shape of the brain. Scientists can tell from this what parts of the brain were well developed, and so which senses were the most essential to the dinosaur.

◄ ANIMAL SENSES

With a modern animal, it is possible to tell something about its senses by simply looking at it. This iguana has eyes on the side of its head, so it has good all-round vision. However, its eyes do not work together to allow it to see in three dimensions. Its ear drum is large, so it may have a good sense of hearing. The nostrils are prominent, so it probably has a sense of smell. It also has brightly coloured skin in the mating season to attract a female, which suggests that the species can see in colour.

Eyes on side of head to spot danger more easily

Large ear drum

Prominent nostril

Skin is coloured bright green in mating season

IGUANA,
A MODERN LIZARD

MAKING NOISES

PARASAUROLOPHUS SKULL

Crest is a folded tube of nose bones

Nostril

Eye socket

Position of ear

In the Cretaceous, a very interesting group of dinosaurs, the hadrosaurs ("duckbilled dinosaurs"), used their skulls to communicate. It seems very likely that the duckbills had a good sense of hearing, because the skulls look as though they belonged to animals that made plenty of noise. *Parasaurolophus* had a crest that consisted of tubes connected to the nostrils. Scientists' tests show that air blown through the crest would have made a noise like a trombone. Duckbills with no crests may have had a flap of skin over their broad beaks that was inflated to make a noise, like the throat-pouch of a bullfrog.

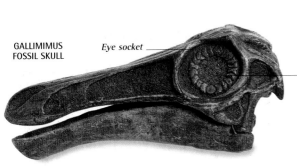

GALLIMIMUS FOSSIL SKULL

Eye socket —

Sclerotic ring

▲ EYE SOCKETS

Some dinosaurs, particularly those with big eyes like *Gallimimus*, had a ring of tiny bones inside the eye. This is called the sclerotic ring. Many modern birds have this. It helps to support the eye and also helps it to focus or pinpoint something it is looking at. Sea reptiles of the Mesozoic had heavy sclerotic rings to protect their eyes from the pressure of the water. Dinosaurs that had a sclerotic ring probably had very sharp eyesight.

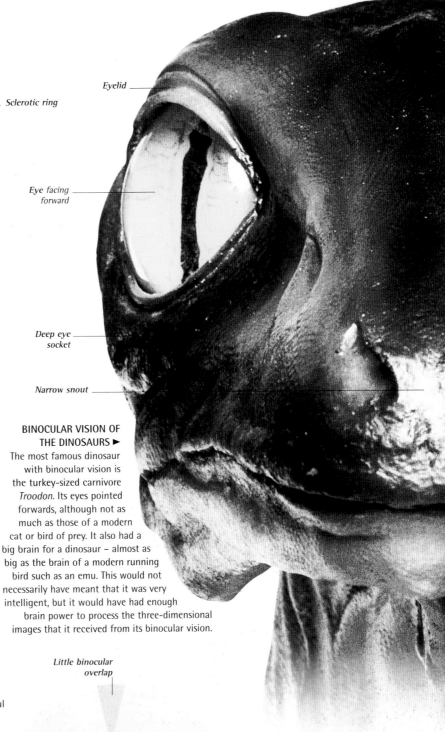

Eyelid —

Eye facing forward —

Deep eye socket —

Narrow snout —

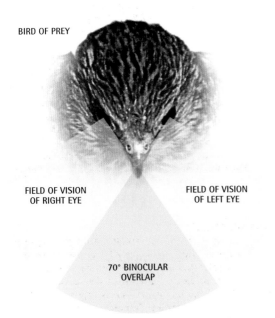

BIRD OF PREY

FIELD OF VISION OF RIGHT EYE

FIELD OF VISION OF LEFT EYE

70° BINOCULAR OVERLAP

▲ BINOCULAR VISION OF MODERN ANIMALS

Hunting animals like birds of prey and people can see in three dimensions. Look at an object with only one eye, then the other. The object's position will appear to change slightly. A person's brain, and that of a bird of prey, can compare the binocular (two-eyed) images and use them to work out how far away the object is – useful if the object is moving prey. Several of the hunting dinosaurs may have had this ability.

BINOCULAR VISION OF THE DINOSAURS ▶

The most famous dinosaur with binocular vision is the turkey-sized carnivore *Troodon*. Its eyes pointed forwards, although not as much as those of a modern cat or bird of prey. It also had a big brain for a dinosaur – almost as big as the brain of a modern running bird such as an emu. This would not necessarily have meant that it was very intelligent, but it would have had enough brain power to process the three-dimensional images that it received from its binocular vision.

Little binocular overlap

FIELD OF VISION OF LEFT EYE

FIELD OF VISION OF RIGHT EYE

senses

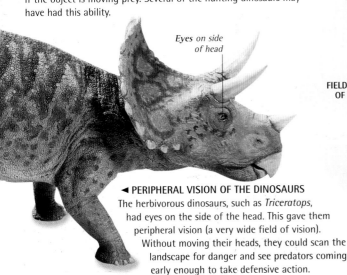

Eyes on side of head

◀ PERIPHERAL VISION OF THE DINOSAURS

The herbivorous dinosaurs, such as *Triceratops*, had eyes on the side of the head. This gave them peripheral vision (a very wide field of vision). Without moving their heads, they could scan the landscape for danger and see predators coming early enough to take defensive action.

◀ PERIPHERAL VISION OF MODERN ANIMALS

A herbivore such as a horse does not need binocular vision. It finds it more useful to have a wide view of everything around it – mainly so that it can see any danger coming while it is eating. That is why a horse's eyes are on the side the head and not pointing forwards. It does not see in colour, but it can see the difference between light and shade.

GROWING UP

Some of the most exciting fossil finds over the last fifty years have been those that have something to do with young dinosaurs – their nests, eggs, or skeletons. When skeletons are found as part of a herd or as a nesting group, it is much easier to tell the young from the adults. The size of a dinosaur's head, eyes, and feet can give clues. The bone itself, if well-enough preserved, sometimes has textures and structures that show different growth rates.

▼ COMPLETE BABY

For a time, the prosauropod *Mussaurus* ("mouse lizard") was thought to be the smallest dinosaur known. Then scientists realized that the skeletons that had been found were all of young hatchlings. The skeletons found were only 18 cm (9 ins) long and could have fitted in a person's hand. The adults would in fact have been about 3 m (10 ft). Some of the bones of the hatchlings had not developed fully, and like most young animals, the skull, eye sockets, and feet were big for the size of the animal.

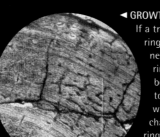

*Big head
with large
eye sockets*

*Large feet
in proportion to
rest of body*

LIFESIZE SKELETON OF
A MUSSAURUS HATCHLING

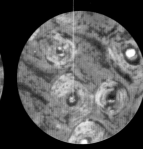

*Growing bone
surrounding blood vessels*

*Blood vessels
(vascular canals)*

SECTION OF BABY THEROPOD BONE   SECTION OF ADULT THEROPOD BONE

▲ DEVELOPING BONE TISSUE

Some dinosaur bones are so well preserved that it is possible to see their structure through a microscope. Like modern animals, the bones of dinosaurs consisted of living tissue, with blood vessels passing through and a space for bone marrow at the centre. Sometimes, when families of dinosaurs are unearthed, it is possible to look at different ages of the same species. Examinations of bones like these has shown that the bones of theropod dinosaurs grew throughout their lives, unlike mammal bones which reach a particular age and then stop growing.

◄ GROWTH RINGS

If a tree is cut down, an examination of the trunk will show rings in the wood from the core of the tree to the bark. Each new ring represents a year of growth of the living tree. The rings are known as growth rings. Sometimes this effect can be seen in dinosaur bones as well. However, it is not possible to simply count the rings to tell what age the dinosaur was when it died. Often the structure of the older bone will have changed during the lifetime of the animal, and the growth rings that were formed earlier will have disappeared.

*Lines showing
a yearly growth*

SECTION OF A TYRANNOSAURUS BONE

STAGES OF GROWTH

Herds of the horned dinosaur *Protoceratops* roamed the Cretaceous plains of Asia like flocks of sheep. Hundreds of fossils of these dinosaurs have been found buried in desert sandstones. They were probably overwhelmed and suffocated in the sandstorms of the period. The remains are at all stages of growth, showing that they moved about in herds or in family groups. The fossils provide very good evidence of how this species developed as they grew older. For example, the skulls and jaws developed at different rates between the time that the *Protoceratops* hatched and the time it reached full adulthood.

*Beak gets
longer and frill
is formed on
top of head*

*Bone of frill
develops as the
animal grows*

*Eye socket in skull
of a newly hatched
Protoceratops*

*As animal grows,
features such as beak
become more distinctive*

growing

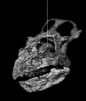

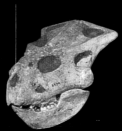

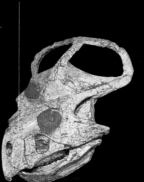

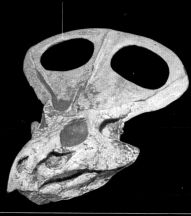

▼ PARENTAL CARE

Dinosaurs like this herbivorous dinosaur, *Leaellynasaura*, probably
nested together in large groups. After the eggs hatched, the adults
would have cared for the hatchlings until they were big enough
to fend for themselves. We know the rates at which ornithopods
like these grew from the bones found at nesting sites. The
hatchlings grew very quickly for a few months. Then, for six
years or so, the juveniles would still be growing fast. By the
time they reached adulthood, the growth rate would have
slowed down or stopped completely. This growth rate
is very like that of modern birds.

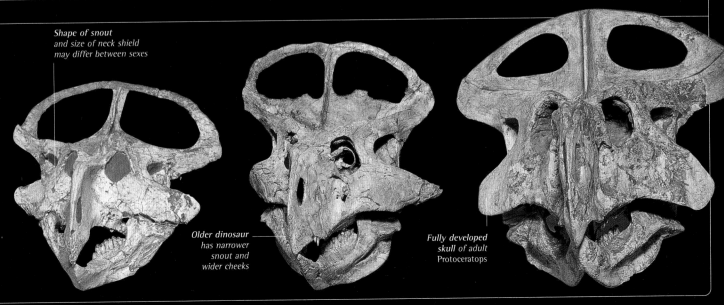

*Shape of snout
and size of neck shield
may differ between sexes*

*Older dinosaur
has narrower
snout and
wider cheeks*

*Fully developed
skull of adult*
Protoceratops

DEATH AND DISEASE

Few dinosaurs reached old age. These creatures were constantly at risk from the environment and from other animals. Many dinosaur species are known only from fossils of juveniles that died before they could become adults. Some dinosaurs died in fights, some starved, some became diseased, and some died from injury. What is known about dinosaur illnesses is very limited. Only if a disease affected the bone is there any direct fossilized proof of what kind of illness it could have been. The study of such events is called palaeopathology.

death

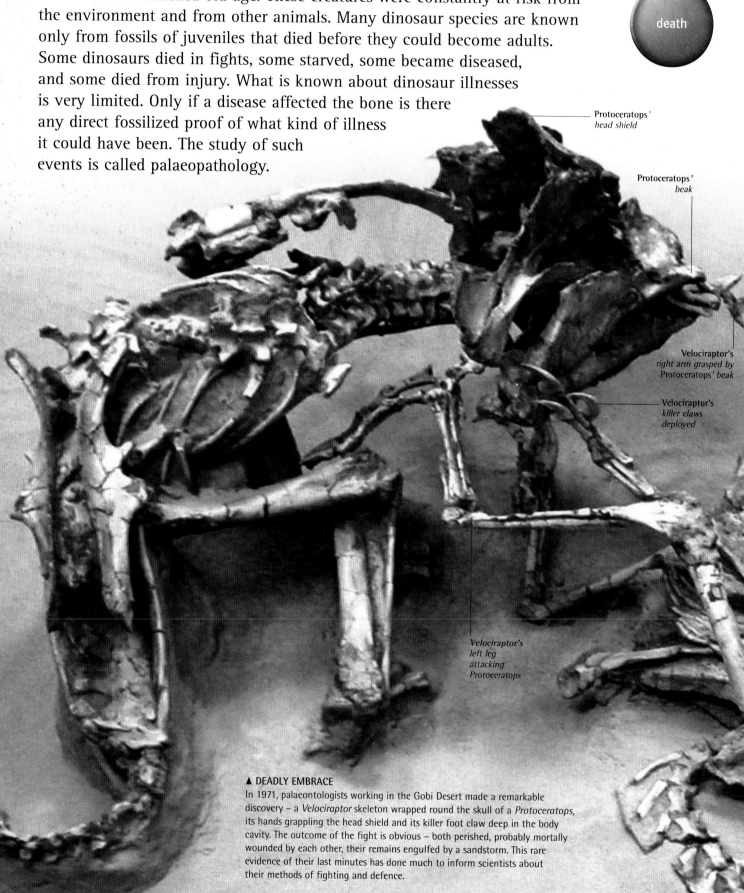

Protoceratops' head shield

Protoceratops' beak

Velociraptor's right arm grasped by Protoceratops' beak

Velociraptor's killer claws deployed

Velociraptor's left leg attacking Protoceratops

▲ DEADLY EMBRACE
In 1971, palaeontologists working in the Gobi Desert made a remarkable discovery – a Velociraptor skeleton wrapped round the skull of a Protoceratops, its hands grappling the head shield and its killer foot claw deep in the body cavity. The outcome of the fight is obvious – both perished, probably mortally wounded by each other, their remains engulfed by a sandstorm. This rare evidence of their last minutes has done much to inform scientists about their methods of fighting and defence.

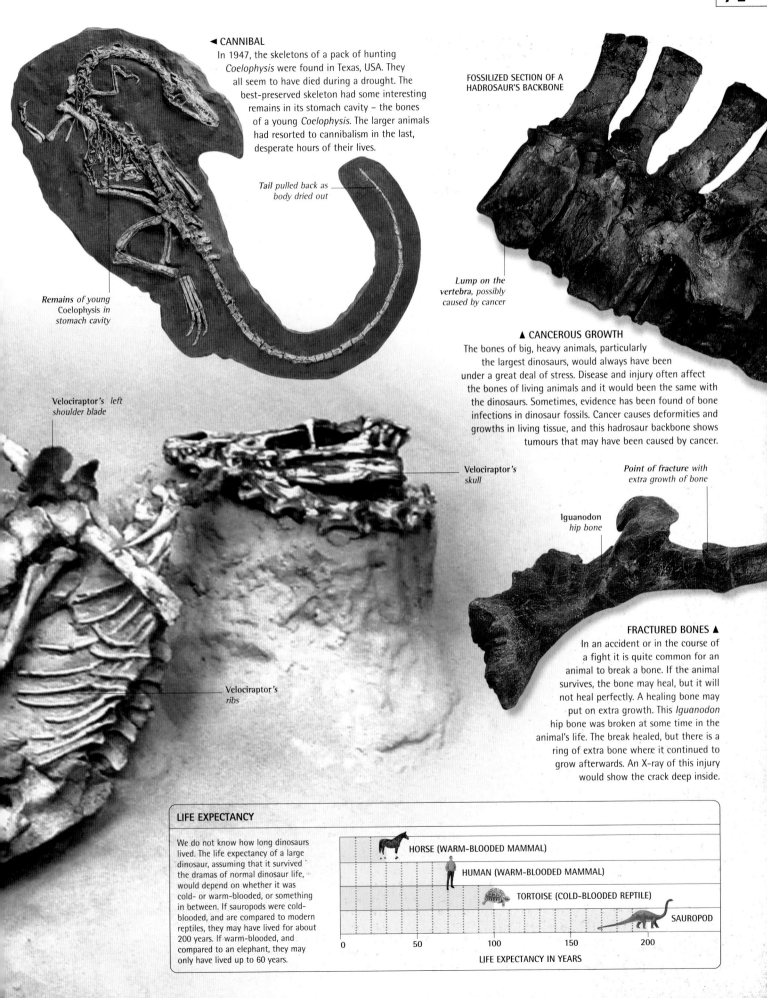

◄ CANNIBAL

In 1947, the skeletons of a pack of hunting *Coelophysis* were found in Texas, USA. They all seem to have died during a drought. The best-preserved skeleton had some interesting remains in its stomach cavity – the bones of a young *Coelophysis*. The larger animals had resorted to cannibalism in the last, desperate hours of their lives.

Tail pulled back as body dried out

FOSSILIZED SECTION OF A HADROSAUR'S BACKBONE

Remains of young Coelophysis in stomach cavity

Lump on the vertebra, possibly caused by cancer

▲ CANCEROUS GROWTH

The bones of big, heavy animals, particularly the largest dinosaurs, would always have been under a great deal of stress. Disease and injury often affect the bones of living animals and it would been the same with the dinosaurs. Sometimes, evidence has been found of bone infections in dinosaur fossils. Cancer causes deformities and growths in living tissue, and this hadrosaur backbone shows tumours that may have been caused by cancer.

Velociraptor's left shoulder blade

Velociraptor's skull

Point of fracture with extra growth of bone

Iguanodon hip bone

Velociraptor's ribs

FRACTURED BONES ▲

In an accident or in the course of a fight it is quite common for an animal to break a bone. If the animal survives, the bone may heal, but it will not heal perfectly. A healing bone may put on extra growth. This *Iguanodon* hip bone was broken at some time in the animal's life. The break healed, but there is a ring of extra bone where it continued to grow afterwards. An X-ray of this injury would show the crack deep inside.

LIFE EXPECTANCY

We do not know how long dinosaurs lived. The life expectancy of a large dinosaur, assuming that it survived the dramas of normal dinosaur life, would depend on whether it was cold- or warm-blooded, or something in between. If sauropods were cold-blooded, and are compared to modern reptiles, they may have lived for about 200 years. If warm-blooded, and compared to an elephant, they may only have lived up to 60 years.

HORSE (WARM-BLOODED MAMMAL)

HUMAN (WARM-BLOODED MAMMAL)

TORTOISE (COLD-BLOODED REPTILE)

SAUROPOD

| 0 | 50 | 100 | 150 | 200 |

LIFE EXPECTANCY IN YEARS

PACK HUNTERS

Just as modern meat-eating animals such as lions combine forces to pull down animals larger than themselves, many flesh-eating theropods hunted in packs. Roaming in gangs, heavily muscled, and armed with vicious claws and powerful jaws lined with sharp teeth, they were intelligent enough to band together before going into the attack. Like some sophisticated hunters today, dinosaurs may have developed tactics to outsmart their prey, such as luring them into traps or surrounding them before the attack.

▲ FAMILY FEASTING
Lions are sociable animals that live together in prides of a dozen or more, including several lionesses and their cubs. They hunt together and later feast on the spoils as a group. Packs of small, carnivorous dinosaurs may have shared larger prey in this way. There was no need for them to defend the kill from the attentions of scavengers as it was quickly devoured. They were then free to move on to their next victim.

Deep wounds are inflicted by sharp teeth and claws

Attacking Allosaurus slashes at the prey's flank from a safe position

ATTACK ON A CAMARASAURUS ▼
A lone, plant-eating *Camarasaurus*, separated from the safety of its herd, had neither the killer instincts nor the sharp weaponry to ward off an attack by two hunting *Allosaurus*. The predators were powerful and agile, able to leap high onto the back of their prey and inflict deep wounds to its head, neck, and spine with their teeth and claws. They continued to slash at the dinosaur until it succumbed from either loss of blood or exhaustion.

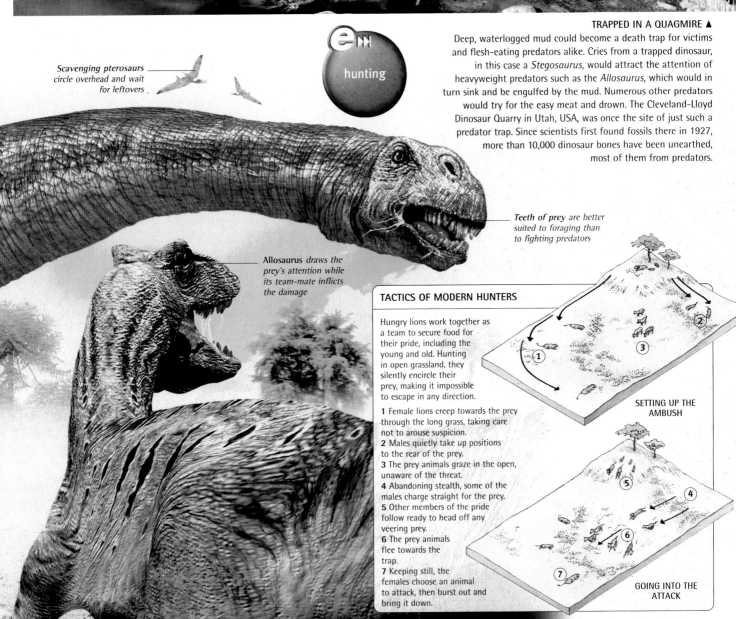

Scavenging pterosaurs circle overhead and wait for leftovers

hunting

TRAPPED IN A QUAGMIRE ▲

Deep, waterlogged mud could become a death trap for victims and flesh-eating predators alike. Cries from a trapped dinosaur, in this case a *Stegosaurus*, would attract the attention of heavyweight predators such as the *Allosaurus*, which would in turn sink and be engulfed by the mud. Numerous other predators would try for the easy meat and drown. The Cleveland-Lloyd Dinosaur Quarry in Utah, USA, was once the site of just such a predator trap. Since scientists first found fossils there in 1927, more than 10,000 dinosaur bones have been unearthed, most of them from predators.

Teeth of prey are better suited to foraging than to fighting predators

Allosaurus draws the prey's attention while its team-mate inflicts the damage

TACTICS OF MODERN HUNTERS

Hungry lions work together as a team to secure food for their pride, including the young and old. Hunting in open grassland, they silently encircle their prey, making it impossible to escape in any direction.

1 Female lions creep towards the prey through the long grass, taking care not to arouse suspicion.
2 Males quietly take up positions to the rear of the prey.
3 The prey animals graze in the open, unaware of the threat.
4 Abandoning stealth, some of the males charge straight for the prey.
5 Other members of the pride follow ready to head off any veering prey.
6 The prey animals flee towards the trap.
7 Keeping still, the females choose an animal to attack, then burst out and bring it down.

SETTING UP THE AMBUSH

GOING INTO THE ATTACK

HUNTER OR SCAVENGER?

Tyrannosaurus was the biggest, fiercest, most formidable hunting animal that ever lived. Or was it? Although it looks like a terrifying predator, and its teeth, jaws, and eyesight seem to confirm that it was, other features such as the muscles and bones suggest that it was a slow mover, unable to run fast after prey. Perhaps *Tyrannosaurus* used different techniques when it needed to find its food. It may have hunted by running in short spurts and catching slow-moving prey. It may have scavenged on dead animals caught by other, speedier theropods, simply scaring them away as they tried to eat.

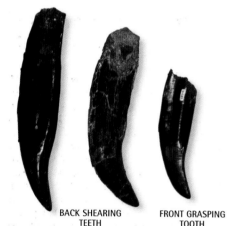

BACK SHEARING TEETH   FRONT GRASPING TOOTH

▲ TEETH

The sharp teeth of a *Tyrannosaurus* suggest that it was a hunter. Those at the front are short, thick, and ideal for clamping into struggling prey and stopping it escaping. The long teeth at the side were thinner, more blade-like, finely serrated on both edges, and curved backwards. This made them perfect for slicing off meat that was already dead. All would have been replaced as they broke off or wore out.

Gaps in skull would have anchored jaw muscles

Sharp teeth were replaced by new ones when damaged

Hinge could open jaw wide

▲ AWESOME JAWS

The muscles that powered the jaws of *Tyrannosaurus* were immense. They would have been strong enough to grip a big animal, tear it limb from limb, and crush the bones. Scientists have found *Tyrannosaurus* tooth marks in the broken bones of horned dinosaurs. The volume of the mouth shows that it could have swallowed up to 227 kg (500 lb) of flesh at a single gulp. Such jaws could have been used by either a hunter or a scavenger.

CARNIVORE ▶

This dinosaur was made for meat-eating – just like the other theropods. Its long jaws housed rows of sharp teeth. Its long hind legs were strong. Its body was relatively small, and was balanced by a heavy tail. But it is difficult to tell if the meat *Tyrannosaurus* ate came from prey that it hunted for itself, or from already dead animals that it found. Its fearsome teeth look like those of a killer, but its sheer size suggests that it was too big and clumsy for hunting.

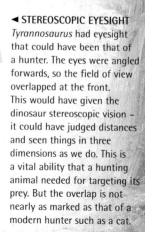

Field of view overlap

FIELD OF VIEW OF LEFT EYE   FIELD OF VIEW OF RIGHT EYE

◀ STEREOSCOPIC EYESIGHT

Tyrannosaurus had eyesight that could have been that of a hunter. The eyes were angled forwards, so the field of view overlapped at the front. This would have given the dinosaur stereoscopic vision – it could have judged distances and seen things in three dimensions as we do. This is a vital ability that a hunting animal needed for targeting its prey. But the overlap is not nearly as marked as that of a modern hunter such as a cat.

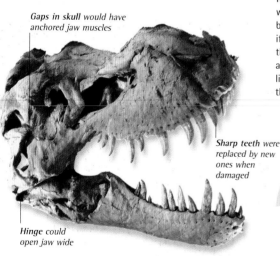

AVAILABILITY OF FOOD FOR SCAVENGING

In nature, a dead animal is a rich source of food. The flesh, internal organs, and even the marrow of the bones are all highly nutritious. Whenever a source of food exists, something will evolve to exploit it. In modern times, dead animals are not left for long – they are soon eaten by scavenging animals. It must have been the same in the Age of Dinosaurs. Living creatures, including *Tyrannosaurus* and other dinosaurs, would have scavenged the corpses of dead dinosaurs.

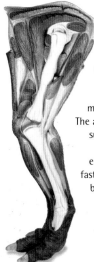

◄ LEG MUSCLES

The evidence provided by the legs of a *Tyrannosaurus* have not helped scientists decide whether this animal was a hunter or not. Its leg bones were huge, and perhaps too massive for it to be a fast runner. The amount of muscle also seems to suggest that it was a slow mover because there was simply not enough muscle to allow it to run fast. All this would argue against it being an active hunter. However, the way the bones are jointed suggests that they were designed to be moved quickly. So the evidence found so far is contradictory.

▲ MODERN HUNTERS AND SCAVENGERS

Although we think of hyenas (seen here on the right) as scavenging animals, they do not always eat animals that are already dead. Hyenas sometimes hunt in packs and bring down swift prey. Likewise, we think of lions (left) as being the ultimate hunting machines. However, lions often scavenge, eating prey that has been killed by another animal. The line between hunting and scavenging is not always clear. Perhaps, back in the Cretaceous, *Tyrannosaurus* adopted both techniques, hunting when necessary, and scavenging corpses when it found them.

T rex

TYRANNOSAURUS PROFILE

Fast or slow? Predator or scavenger? Either way, *Tyrannosaurus* was one of the biggest carnivores ever to have stalked the Earth.

Height: 6.5 m (22 ft)

Length: 12.8 m (42 ft)

Weight: Up to 6.4 tonnes (up to 7 US tons)

Leg length: 2.5 m (8 ft)

Stride length: 3.7–4.6 m (2–15 ft)

Estimated top speed: 8–72 kph (5–45 mph)

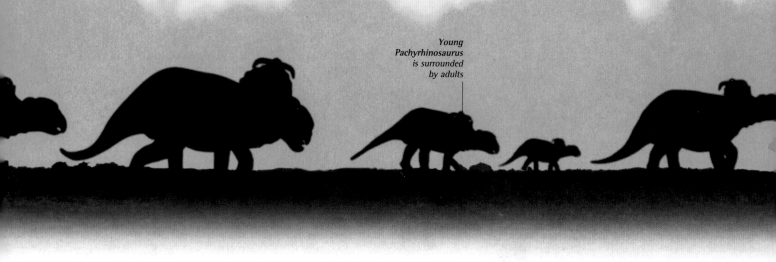

Young Pachyrhinosaurus is surrounded by adults

HERDING DINOSAURS

Travelling as a herd provides safety in numbers because it is difficult for a hungry predator to pick out just one animal for slaughter. Group members can also warn each other if there are flesh-eaters on the prowl. It is possible that, for these reasons, some plant-eating dinosaurs formed herds. We know that certain dinosaurs travelled in groups because large clusters of their fossil bones and footprints have been found together. These dinosaurs may also have trudged vast distances together to find good grazing land and breeding sites. These journeys are called migrations. Today, many animals follow a herding life for much the same reasons as their ancient ancestors.

e ▶▶ herds

Footprints show the direction of travel

◄ PRESERVED IN STONE
Found on the Colorado Plateau in western USA, these fossilized footprints consist of tracks made by a number of *Apatosaurus*. Multiple tracks provide evidence that some dinosaurs travelled together in herds. Scientists analysing such trackways have also found that, in some cases, smaller, juvenile footprints overprint those made by the adults. From this we know the older, stronger dinosaurs led the herds, while the young ones either followed at the rear or marched along in the middle, protected at the front and back by the adults.

Larger footprints belong to the adults

Smaller footprints belong to the young

Adult dinosaur enjoys the protection of the herd

▲ BOUND FOR THE ARCTIC

In Late Cretaceous times, herds of *Pachyrhinosaurus* migrated north from what is now Alberta, Canada, to the Arctic. Feeding on large-leafed plants, they remained there until driven south again by the bitterly cold winter. We know they made these epic treks because fossils of this lumbering herbivore have been discovered in Alberta and 3,500 km (2,200 miles) away in northern Alaska, USA.

◄ HAZARDOUS JOURNEYS

Long journeys can prove hazardous for migrating animals because predators lurk at every turn. Travelling in search of fresh grass, wildebeest migrate distances of up to 2,900 km (1,800 miles) through Tanzania and Kenya. They often risk attack by crocodiles as they cross rivers. It is likely migrating dinosaurs would have faced similar dangers, perhaps also falling victim to crocodilians.

DINOSAUR HIGHWAY

1,000 km

☐ *Cretaceous land*
↖ *Modern borders*
↖ *Modern coastline*
♣ *Footprint sites*

In Cretaceous times, the whole of North America was divided by a vast sea, called the Western Interior Seaway (shown in blue). The present-day fossil footprint sites on this map show a migration route to northern Alaska along the western edge of the seaway, in the shadow of the Rocky Mountains. These *Iguanodon* footprints were made in the wet, coastal sediments. They eventually hardened to rock, preserving in stone the evidence for migratory behaviour in some North American dinosaurs.

Adult musk oxen face outwards towards threats

▲ DEFENSIVE CIRCLE

Dinosaur herds may have used group defence tactics to protect themselves from predators. *Triceratops* could have formed a circle and faced an attacker with their three fearsome horns and bony frills. Any predator rash enough to approach may have been driven off by a charging adult. At full tilt, *Triceratops* may have been able to run at a speed of 25 kph (15 mph). This could have deterred even *Tyrannosaurus*.

▲ CHILD REARING

Like *Triceratops*, this group of musk oxen keep their young within a close, protective circle. The threat of predators is not the only reason for this behaviour. Older members of the herd are at hand to lead by example and teach the young how to survive and grow into adulthood. It is quite likely that some of the adults in a herd of dinosaurs also took responsibility for the rearing and education of their young.

NESTING COLONIES

Ever since dinosaurs were identified as reptiles, scientists have assumed that they laid eggs, in the same way that most modern reptiles lay eggs. This was confirmed when the first dinosaur eggs and nests were found in the Gobi Desert, Mongolia, in the 1920s. Since then many more finds have been made – most importantly the discovery of a nesting colony of *Maiasaura* in Montana, USA. Many nesting sites show evidence of bird-like behaviour that adds weight to the theory of some scientists that birds evolved from feathered dinosaurs.

▼ FAMILY LIFE

In the 1970s, at a place named Egg Mountain in Montana, USA, a whole colony of fossilized hadrosaur nests was found. They belonged to a dinosaur called *Maiasaura*. The nests had been made of mud, and were about 1 m (3 ft) high, with a bowl-like depression in the top. It is thought that migrating herds of *Maiasaura* returned to this mass breeding ground year after year to lay their eggs and raise their young.

nests

Young Maiasaura *grew to around 3 m (10 ft) in one year*

◄ HATCHING OUT

There were many different fossils at the Montana site. Egg shells in the nest showed where the eggs had hatched. The bones of hatchlings revealed that some of the babies did not survive the first few days. The bones of older youngsters showed that the young remained at the nesting site for a long time before becoming independent. It seems the parents looked after them in the same way as birds care for their young, feeding and caring for them until they are ready to leave.

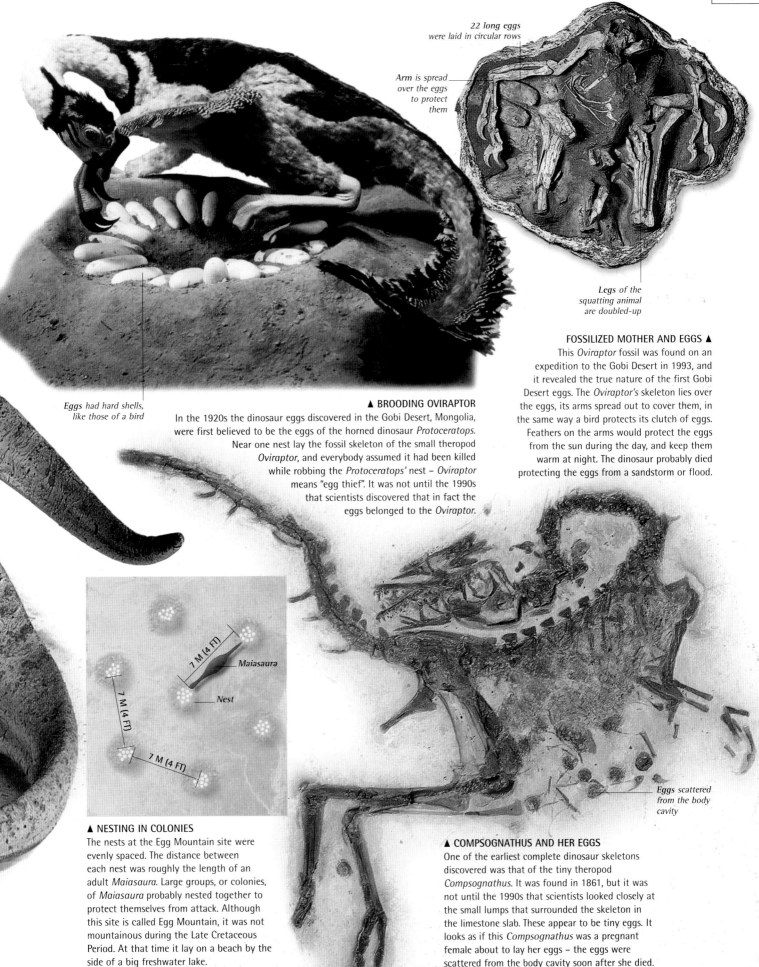

*22 long eggs
were laid in circular rows*

*Arm is spread
over the eggs
to protect
them*

*Legs of the
squatting animal
are doubled-up*

FOSSILIZED MOTHER AND EGGS ▲
This *Oviraptor* fossil was found on an
expedition to the Gobi Desert in 1993, and
it revealed the true nature of the first Gobi
Desert eggs. The *Oviraptor's* skeleton lies over
the eggs, its arms spread out to cover them, in
the same way a bird protects its clutch of eggs.
Feathers on the arms would protect the eggs
from the sun during the day, and keep them
warm at night. The dinosaur probably died
protecting the eggs from a sandstorm or flood.

*Eggs had hard shells,
like those of a bird*

▲ BROODING OVIRAPTOR
In the 1920s the dinosaur eggs discovered in the Gobi Desert, Mongolia,
were first believed to be the eggs of the horned dinosaur *Protoceratops*.
Near one nest lay the fossil skeleton of the small theropod
Oviraptor, and everybody assumed it had been killed
while robbing the *Protoceratops'* nest – *Oviraptor*
means "egg thief". It was not until the 1990s
that scientists discovered that in fact the
eggs belonged to the *Oviraptor*.

7 M (4 FT)

Maiasaura

7 M (4 FT)

Nest

7 M (4 FT)

*Eggs scattered
from the body
cavity*

▲ NESTING IN COLONIES
The nests at the Egg Mountain site were
evenly spaced. The distance between
each nest was roughly the length of an
adult *Maiasaura*. Large groups, or colonies,
of *Maiasaura* probably nested together to
protect themselves from attack. Although
this site is called Egg Mountain, it was not
mountainous during the Late Cretaceous
Period. At that time it lay on a beach by the
side of a big freshwater lake.

▲ COMPSOGNATHUS AND HER EGGS
One of the earliest complete dinosaur skeletons
discovered was that of the tiny theropod
Compsognathus. It was found in 1861, but it was
not until the 1990s that scientists looked closely at
the small lumps that surrounded the skeleton in
the limestone slab. These appear to be tiny eggs. It
looks as if this *Compsognathus* was a pregnant
female about to lay her eggs – the eggs were
scattered from the body cavity soon after she died.

CHANGING FACES

No one has ever seen a living dinosaur, so scientists rely on fossil remains to provide clues to how these ancient reptiles looked and behaved when they were alive. Scrappy evidence in the past meant the early dinosaur experts had certain beliefs about dinosaurs we now know to be incorrect. New discoveries are being made all the time, and each one expands what we know about dinosaurs – sometimes confirming, and sometimes over-turning, the accepted thinking about a particular species. Examples of the changing faces of certain dinosaurs are shown on these pages.

▼ FIERCE, BUT FLUFFY

One of the most significant leaps in how we think dinosaurs looked has happened since the mid-1990s. Before then it was thought that, because dinosaurs were reptiles, they all had scaly skin. Many scientists no longer believe this to be the case for all dinosaurs, based on fossils found in China. The evidence suggests that some small predators, such as *Velociraptor* had bodies clothed in feathers and down. These coverings are usually associated with birds, so the finds provide evidence supporting the theory that dinosaurs and birds are related.

VELOCIRAPTOR WITHOUT FUR AND FEATHERS

◄ DOWN FROM THE TREES

The first *Hypsilophodon* fossils were discovered in 1849, on the Isle of Wight, England. At the time, it was believed this small, agile, plant-eating dinosaur had lived in trees, where it used its long tail for balancing on branches, and its sharp claws for clinging on. This theory has now been proved completely wrong. Today, scientists believe *Hypsilophodon* was actually a ground-living dinosaur, which held its stiff tail off the ground, using it as a stabilizer as it moved. It probably used its clawed hands to pull at the plants it ate.

Tail held off the ground

Featherless legs lessen air-resistance and help *Velociraptor run faster*

Hands are too feeble to cling on to branches

HYPSILOPHODON ON THE GROUND

◄ OUT OF THE SWAMP
Ideas about *Corythosaurus's* lifestyle have altered over recent years. These changing views are based on theories about the function of its head crest. As it was hollow, the crest was once thought to be an underwater breathing tube used like a snorkel. This led scientists to believe *Corythosaurus* lived in water. It is now thought that *Corythosaurus* was a land animal, and that its crest was either for display, or a sound chamber through which it made noises.

CORYTHOSAURUS IN A SWAMP

CORYTHOSAURUS ON DRY LAND

Large skull *with a big brain, making* Velociraptor *an intelligent predator*

Long, slender *jaws for poking inside a carcass and grabbing at flesh*

Small, sharp *biting teeth*

Colour of face, body, and *feathers can only be guessed at*

VELOCIRAPTOR WITH FEATHERS

Soft, fluffy down *and feathers covered the body*

Curved toe claw *grew on the second toe of each foot*

Fingers *ended in long, sharp claws*

theories

IGUANODON OVER TIME

1850S IGUANODON
In 1853, British sculptor Benjamin Waterhouse Hawkins created a concrete model of an *Iguanodon.* Guided by Sir Richard Owen, the sculptor showed the dinosaur as a heavily built quadruped with a horn on the tip of its nose.

Snout horn

1880S IGUANODON
Fossil skeletons found at Bernissart, Belgium, revised the view of this dinosaur radically. *Iguanodon* no longer had a nose horn, and it was depicted in a strictly bipedal, kangaroo-like posture, but with its tail dragging on the ground.

Tail on *ground*

PRESENT-DAY IGUANODON
It is now believed *Iguanodon* held its heavy tail off the ground, using it to counter-balance the weight of its body. It might not have been strictly bipedal as once imagined. Recent studies show it could move on either two or four legs.

Tail off *ground*

DINOSAURS ON DISPLAY

Dinosaur displays in museums can take many forms. Original fossils are shown in glass cases, often presented in the rock in which they are embedded. Complete dinosaur skeletons can be mounted to give a more three-dimensional impression of the animal, and to show its scale and structure. A mounted skeleton is called a reconstruction. There are also displays that show what a dinosaur was like when alive, such as a painting, or a model of a dinosaur set in the environment it would have lived in. This is called a restoration.

Long, stiff tail helped the dinosaur to balance while running and leaping

Mounting framework lies inside the replica bones, and is invisible

Bird-like feet with terrifying hooked claws for tearing prey apart

Skeleton is so light it can be fixed to the floor at only one point

THE DIFFERENT FUNCTIONS OF A MUSEUM

FOSSIL STORE
The majority of dinosaur fossils are never put on display. They are kept in the storerooms of museums and universities where they are available for scientists. Sometimes this is because they are too valuable or fragile to be displayed in public. Often, it is because they do not look impressive. Only the most spectacular exhibits are put on show. Fossils may also be too heavy or fragile to mount, so some exhibits are made up of copies cast from the original bones.

LAB ON VIEW
In some modern museums the preparation laboratories have a viewing gallery so that the public can see the technicians and palaeontologists at work. This helps to show that the study of dinosaurs is going on all the time, and demonstrates the enormous amount of work involved in palaeontology. Sometimes, the public can also meet palaeontologists and ask them questions.

TRADITIONAL DISPLAY
A mounted skeleton with the original fossilized bones, assembled on a sturdy steel framework, has been the traditional way to display dinosaur fossils in museums. They still give a dramatic impression of the scale and structure of these incredible animals. In the past, fossils were covered in a dark, tarry varnish to preserve them, but this is not done today as it hides many of the details.

Curved spine, as
the dinosaur twists
and turns, suggests
speed and mobility

Lightweight skull
needs little support

Jaws lined with
the large, sharp
teeth of a hunter

*Long, thin
front limbs*
with lethal
grasping claws

museums

▲ RECONSTRUCTION

This sickle-clawed dromaeosaur
skeleton has been mounted to show
the dinosaur in action, rather than
in the more traditional standing pose.
Dromaeosaur means "running lizard",
and it was an aggressive hunter.
This is dramatically conveyed by the
positions of the legs and the gaping
jaws. A mount like this uses replicas
of the original bones, made in a sturdy
but lightweight material, which are
much easier to handle and mount.

◄ RESTORATION

Some museums have full-scale
models that are able to move as
if they were alive. The flesh of this
Allosaurus hides a whole array of
animatronics – robotic mechanisms
that make the arms move, the jaws
open and close, the eyes blink, and
the rib-cage expand and contract,
as if the animal were breathing. Such
models are often equipped with sound
devices to make them even more
realistic. Some even smell – to convey
the foul breath of a carnivorous
dinosaur with pieces of rotten
meat trapped in its teeth.

EVOLUTION

When young animals grow up, they may be similar to their parents but they are never identical. If one animal is able to move faster than another of the same species, it can probably catch more prey and be better fed. It is more likely to be healthy and to attract a mate. Its ability to move fast will probably be passed down to its young, and to their young. Over many generations, the species will evolve (change) to become superb hunters. This process, known as natural selection, was first described by Charles Darwin in the 19th century and explains the way that life on Earth has evolved from the earliest times.

evolution

Time	Era	Period	Name	Description	
4,600–545 MYA			PRECAMBRIAN	Origin of life and evolution of Vendian organisms	Mawsonites, Collenia
545–490 MYA	PALAEOZOIC ERA		CAMBRIAN	Single-celled and multi-cellular life appear in the seas	Olenellus
490–445 MYA			ORDOVICIAN	Nautiloids and jawed vertebrates swim in the seas	Orthoceras, Crytoceras
445–415 MYA			SILURIAN	Plants and arachnids grow on land	Baragwanathia, Pseudocrinites
415–355 MYA			DEVONIAN	Vertebrates develop four limbs and digits	Pteraspis
355–290 MYA			CARBONIFEROUS	Reptiles and flying insects populate the land	Sandalodus
290–250 MYA			PERMIAN	Sail-back synapsids roam the Earth	Edaphosaurus, Diplocaulus
250–200 MYA	MESOZOIC ERA		TRIASSIC	First dinosaurs, mammals, turtles, and frogs appear	Lystrosaurus
200–145 MYA			JURASSIC	Pterosaurs fly in the air, dinosaurs rule the land	Pterodactylus, Proceratosaurus
145–65 MYA			CRETACEOUS	Dinosaurs die out, first modern mammals take over	Triceratops
65–53 MYA	CENOZOIC ERA	TERTIARY PERIOD	PALAEOCENE EPOCH	Owls, shrews, and hedgehogs make an appearance	Taeniolabis, Phenacodus
53–33.7 MYA			EOCENE EPOCH	Horses, elephants, dogs, and cats establish themselves	Palaeochiropteryx, Hyracotherium
33.7–23.5 MYA			OLIGOCENE EPOCH	First monkeys, deer, and rhinoceroses arrive on the scene	Phiomia
23.5–5.3 MYA			MIOCENE EPOCH	First apes, mice, and many new mammals appear	Samotherium
5.31–1.64 MYA			PLIOCENE EPOCH	Cattle and sheep are common; whales diversify	Bison, Balaena
1.64–0.01 MYA		QUATERNARY PERIOD	PLEISTOCENE EPOCH	First modern humans appear	Gigantopithecus
0.01 MYA – PRESENT			HOLOCENE EPOCH	Extinctions are caused by human activity	Homo sapiens

CLASSIFICATION

Scientists have developed various systems of classification to describe living things. The one used here is a cladogram, which is a diagram that shows the relationship between different species of animal. Each branch of the cladogram is a clade, which includes an ancestral species and its descendants, showing how a particular group of dinosaurs evolved. Each clade of dinosaurs shared certain characteristics – perhaps they looked alike, moved in a similar way, or had the same habits or lifestyles.

classification

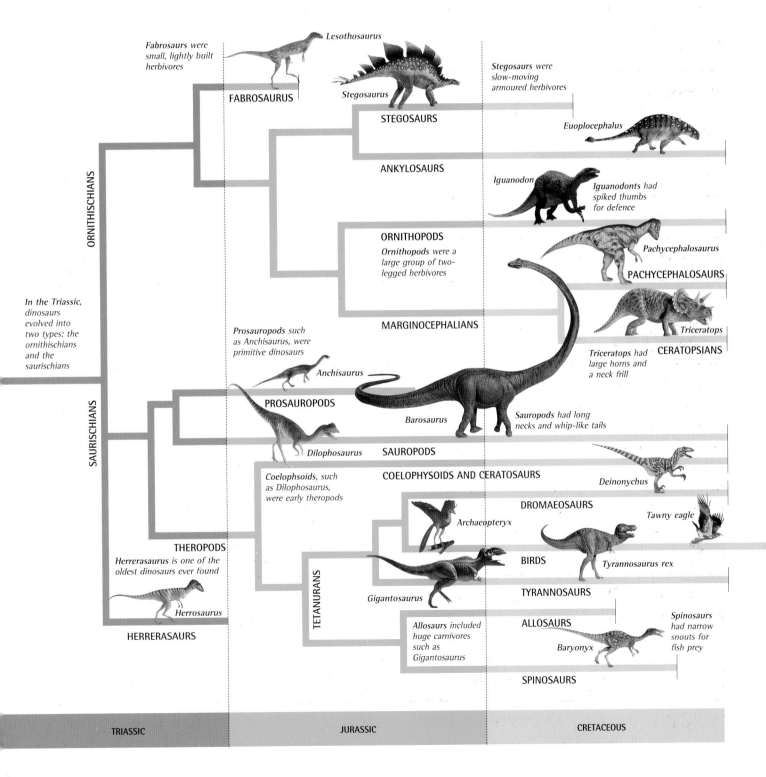

Fabrosaurs were small, lightly built herbivores

Lesothosaurus

FABROSAURUS

Stegosaurus

Stegosaurs were slow-moving armoured herbivores

STEGOSAURS

ANKYLOSAURS

Euoplocephalus

Iguanodon

Iguanodonts had spiked thumbs for defence

ORNITHOPODS

Ornithopods were a large group of two-legged herbivores

Pachycephalosaurus

PACHYCEPHALOSAURS

MARGINOCEPHALIANS

Triceratops

Triceratops had large horns and a neck frill

CERATOPSIANS

Prosauropods such as Anchisaurus, were primitive dinosaurs

Anchisaurus

PROSAUROPODS

Barosaurus

Sauropods had long necks and whip-like tails

Dilophosaurus

SAUROPODS

Coelophsoids, such as Dilophosaurus, were early theropods

COELOPHYSOIDS AND CERATOSAURS

Deinonychus

DROMAEOSAURS

Archaeopteryx

Tawny eagle

BIRDS

Tyrannosaurus rex

THEROPODS

Herrerasaurus is one of the oldest dinosaurs ever found

Gigantosaurus

TYRANNOSAURS

Herrosaurus

HERRERASAURS

Allosaurs included huge carnivores such as Gigantosaurus

ALLOSAURS

Baryonyx

Spinosaurs had narrow snouts for fish prey

SPINOSAURS

ORNITHISCHIANS

SAURISCHIANS

TETANURANS

In the Triassic, dinosaurs evolved into two types: the ornithischians and the saurischians

| TRIASSIC | JURASSIC | CRETACEOUS |

PROFILES

Dinosaur fossils have been found all over the world, and more are being found all the time. Each time a new fossil is examined by a palaeontologist or other scientist, more information is gleaned about how and where the animal lived. The dinosaur profiles on these pages summarize what is known today about the dinosaurs that appear in this book.

profiles

ACANTHOPHOLIS "SPINY SCALES"

Pronunciation: a-KAN-tho-FOLE-is
Maximum length: 4 m (13 ft)
Time: Early Cretaceous
Diet: plants
Habitat: rivers, woodland
Fossil finds: South America (Bolivia), Europe (England)

ALBERTOSAURUS "LIZARD FROM ALBERTA"

Pronunciation: al-BERT-oh-SAW-rus
Maximum length: 8 m (26 ft)
Time: Late Cretaceous
Diet: hunted and scavenged meat
Habitat: open woodland
Fossil finds: North America (USA, Canada)

ALLOSAURUS "DIFFERENT LIZARD"

Pronunciation: AL-oh-SAW-rus
Maximum length: 12 m (39 ft)
Time: Late Jurassic
Diet: meat
Habitat: open countryside
Fossil finds: North America (western USA), Australia

ANCHISAURUS "NEAR LIZARD"

Pronunciation: AN-ki-SAW-rus
Maximum length: 2.5 m (8 ft)
Time: Early Jurassic
Diet: plants
Habitat: dry savannah
Fossil finds: North America (Connecticut, Massachusetts)

ANHANGUERA "OLD DEVIL"

Pronunciation: AN-han-GER-a
Wingspan: 4.5 m (15 ft)
Time: Early Cretaceous
Diet: fish
Habitat: coastal regions
Fossil finds: South America (Brazil)

ANKYLOSAURUS "FUSED LIZARD"

Pronunciation: an-KY-low-SAW-rus
Maximum length: 10.5 m (34 ft)
Time: Late Cretaceous
Diet: plants
Habitat: forests
Fossil finds: North America (Montana, USA; Alberta, Canada), South America (Bolivia)

APATOSAURUS "DECEPTIVE LIZARD"

Pronunciation: a-PAT-oh-SAW-rus
Maximum length: 21 m (69 ft)
Time: Late Jurassic
Diet: plants
Habitat: flood plain
Fossil finds: North America (Oklahoma, Utah, Wyoming)

ARCHAEOPTERYX "ANCIENT WING"

Pronunciation: ar-kee-OP-ter-ix
Wingspan: 0.5 m (1 ft 6 in)
Time: Late Jurassic
Diet: small animals
Habitat: tropical desert islands
Fossil finds: western Europe

BARAPASAURUS "BIG LEG"

Pronunciation: ba-RA-pa-SAW-rus
Maximum length: 18 m (59 ft)
Time: Early Jurassic
Diet: plants
Habitat: low-lying flood plain
Fossil finds: Asia (India)

BAROSAURUS "HEAVY LIZARD"

Pronunciation: BAR-o-SAW-rus
Maximum length: 27 m (89 ft)
Time: Late Jurassic
Diet: plants
Habitat: flood plain
Fossil finds: North America (western USA), Africa (Tanzania)

BARYONYX "HEAVY CLAW"

Pronunciation: BAR-ee-ON-ix
Maximum length: 9.5 m (31 ft)
Time: Early Cretaceous
Diet: fish
Habitat: rivers, woodlands
Fossil finds: Europe (England)

BRACHIOSAURUS "ARMED LIZARD"

Pronunciation: BRACK-ee-oh-SAW-rus
Maximum length: 25 m (82 ft)
Time: Middle to Late Jurassic
Diet: plants
Habitat: open woodland
Fossil finds: Africa (Tanzania), Europe (Portugal), North America

BRACHYLOPHOSAURUS "SHORT-CRESTED LIZARD"

Pronunciation: brack-ee-LOAF-oh-SAW-rus
Maximum length: 7 m (23 ft)
Time: Late Cretaceous
Diet: plants
Habitat: swamps
Fossil finds: North America (Alberta, Canada)

CAMARASAURUS "CHAMBERED LIZARD"

Pronunciation: kam-AR-a-SAW-rus
Maximum length: 18 m (59 ft)
Time: Late Jurassic
Diet: plants
Habitat: flood plain
Fossil finds: North America (Colorado, New Mexico, Utah, Wyoming), Europe (Portugal)

CAMPTOSAURUS "FLEXIBLE LIZARD"

Pronunciation: KAMP-toe-SAW-rus
Maximum length: 7 m (23 ft)
Time: Late Jurassic to Early Cretaceous
Diet: low-lying plants
Habitat: wooded lowlands
Fossil finds: North America (Utah), Europe

CARCHARODONTOSAURUS "SHARK-TOOTHED LIZARD"

Pronunciation: kar-KAR-oh-DONT-oh-SAW-rus
Maximum length: 13.5 m (40 ft)
Time: Early Cretaceous
Diet: hunted and scavenged meat
Habitat: wooded river valleys
Fossil finds: North Africa (Egypt, Morocco, Tunisia, Algeria, Libya, Niger)

CARNOTAURUS "FLESH-EATING"

Pronunciation: KAR-noh-TOR-us
Maximum length: 7.5 m (25 ft)
Time: Middle to Late Cretaceous
Diet: meat
Habitat: arid plains
Fossil finds: South America (Argentina)

CERATOSAURUS "HORNED LIZARD"

Pronunciation: SER-a-toe-SAW-rus
Maximum length: 6 m (20 ft)
Time: Late Jurassic
Diet: hunted and scavenged meat
Habitat: open countryside
Fossil finds: North America (Colorado, Utah), Africa (Tanzania)

COELOPHYSIS "HOLLOW FORM"

Pronunciation: SEEL-oh-FY-sis
Maximum length: 2.8 m (9 ft)
Time: Late Triassic
Diet: reptiles, fish, other dinosaurs
Habitat: dry savannah
Fossil finds: North America (Arizona, Utah, New Mexico)

COMPSOGNATHUS "PRETTY JAW"

Pronunciation: KOMP-sow-NAY-thus
Maximum length: 1.4 m (4 ft 6 in)
Time: Late Jurassic
Diet: insects, lizards, other small animals
Habitat: desert islands
Fossil finds: Europe (Germany, France)

CORYTHOSAURUS "HELMET LIZARD"

Pronunciation: ko-RITH-oh-SAW-rus
Maximum length: 10 m (33 ft)
Time: Late Cretaceous
Diet: low-lying plants
Habitat: forests
Fossil finds: North America (Montana, USA; Alberta, Canada)

CRYOLOPHOSAURUS "FROZEN-CRESTED LIZARD"

Pronunciation: KRIE-ol-lof-oh-SAW-rus
Maximum length: 6 m (20 ft)
Time: Early Jurassic
Diet: hunted prosauropods and other plant-eating dinosaurs
Habitat: moist riverside
Fossil finds: Antarctica

DEINONYCHUS "TERRIBLE CLAW"

Pronunciation: DIE-no-NIKE-us
Maximum length: 3 m (10 ft)
Time: Early Cretaceous
Diet: meat
Habitat: open woodland
Fossil finds: North America (Montana, Utah, Wyoming)

DIPLODOCUS "DOUBLE-BEAMED"

Pronunciation: dip-LOD-oh-kus
Maximum length: 27 m (89 ft)
Time: Late Jurassic
Diet: plants
Habitat: flood plain
Fossil finds: North America (Colorado, Montana, Utah, Wyoming)

DILOPHOSAURUS "TWO-RIDGE LIZARD"

Pronunciation: DYE-lo-fuh-SAW-rus
Maximum length: 6 m (20 ft)
Time: Late Jurassic
Diet: meat
Habitat: scrub and open woodland
Fossil finds: North America (Arizona), China

DROMAEOSAURUS "RUNNING LIZARD"

Pronunciation: DROME-ee-oh-SAW-rus
Maximum length: 1.8 m (6 ft)
Time: Late Cretaceous
Diet: meat, including other dinosaurs
Habitat: open woodland
Fossil finds: North America (Montana, USA; Alberta, Canada)

DRYOSAURUS "OAK TREE LIZARD"

Pronunciation: DRY-oh-SAW-rus
Maximum length: 3 m (10 ft)
Time: Late Jurassic
Diet: low-growing plants
Habitat: forest
Fossil finds: Africa (Tanzania), North America (Colorado, Wyoming)

DSUNGARIPTERUS "JUNGGAR BASIN WING"

Pronunciation: JUNG-gah-RIP-te-rus
Wingspan: 3 m (10 ft)
Time: Early Cretaceous
Diet: fish, molluscs, seashore animals
Habitat: coastal shores
Fossil finds: Asia (China)

EDMONTONIA "FROM EDMONTON"

Pronunciation: ed-MONT-oh-NIA
Maximum length: 7 m (23 ft)
Time: Late Cretaceous
Diet: low-growing plants
Habitat: open woodland
Fossil finds: North America (Alberta in Canada, Alaska, Montana in USA)

EDMONTOSAURUS "EDMONTON LIZARD"

Pronunciation: ed-MONT-oh-SAW-rus
Maximum length: 13 m (43 ft)
Time: Late Cretaceous
Diet: low-lying plants
Habitat: swamps
Fossil finds: North America (Wyoming, Montana, and New Jersey, USA; Alberta, Canada)

ELASMOSAURUS "THIN-PLATED LIZARD"

Pronunciation: ee-LAZ-mo-SAW-rus
Maximum length: 14 m (46 ft)
Time: Late Cretaceous
Diet: fish, swimming molluscs
Habitat: shallow seas
Fossil finds: North America (Wyoming, Kansas), Asia (Japan)

EORAPTOR "DAWN RAPTOR"

Pronunciation: ee-oh-RAP-tor
Maximum length: 1 m (3 ft)
Time: Late Triassic
Diet: hunted and scavenged meat
Habitat: river valleys
Fossil finds: South America (Argentina)

EUOPLOCEPHALUS "WELL-ARMOURED LIZARD"

Pronunciation: you-op-luh-SEF-uh-lus
Maximum length: 7 m (23 ft)
Time: Late Cretaceous
Diet: low-lying plants
Habitat: open woodland
Fossil finds: North America (Montana, USA; Alberta, Canada)

GALLIMIMUS "ROOSTER MIMIC"

Pronunciation: GAL-ih-MIME-us
Maximum length: 6 m (20 ft)
Time: Late Cretaceous
Diet: insects, lizards, eggs, plants
Habitat: river valleys
Fossil finds: Asia (Mongolia)

GASTONIA "FOR GASTON"

Pronunciation: gas-TONE-ia
Maximum length: 5 m (16 ft)
Time: Early Cretaceous
Diet: low-lying plants
Habitat: open woodland
Fossil finds: North America (Utah)

GIGANTOSAURUS "GIANT SOUTHERN LIZARD"

Pronunciation: gi-GANT-oh-SAW-rus
Maximum length: 13 m (43 ft)
Time: Late Cretaceous
Diet: meat
Habitat: flood plain
Fossil finds: South America (Argentina)

HADROSAURUS "BULKY LIZARD"

Pronunciation: HAD-roe-SAW-rus
Maximum length: 10 m (33 ft)
Time: Late Cretaceous
Diet: plants
Habitat: wooded lowlands
Fossil finds: North America (New Jersey, Montana, and New Mexico, USA; Alberta, Canada)

HERRERASAURUS "HERRERA'S LIZARD"

Pronunciation: her-rare-uh-SAW-rus
Maximum length: 4 m (13 ft)
Time: Late Triassic
Diet: meat
Habitat: river valleys
Fossil finds: South America (Argentina)

HETERODONTOSAURUS "DIFFERENT-TOOTHED LIZARD"

Pronunciation: HET-er-oh-DONT-oh-SAW-rus
Maximum length: 1.3 m (4 ft)
Time: Late Triassic to Early Jurassic
Diet: plants
Habitat: dry lowlands
Fossil finds: Africa (South Africa)

HYLAEOSAURUS "WOODLAND LIZARD"

Pronunciation: HY-lee-oh-SAW-rus
Maximum length: 4 m (13 ft)
Time: Early Cretaceous
Diet: plants
Habitat: open woodland
Fossil finds: South America (Bolivia), England

HYPSILOPHODON "HIGH-CRESTED TOOTH"

Pronunciation: hip-see-LOAF-oh-don
Maximum length: 2.3 m (6 ft)
Time: Early Cretaceous
Diet: low-growing plants
Habitat: woodlands
Fossil finds: Europe (UK, Spain, Portugal), North America (South Dakota, USA)

ICHTHYOSAURUS "FISH LIZARD"

Pronunciation: ICK-thee-oh-SAW-rus
Maximum length: 3 m (10 ft)
Time: Early Jurassic to Early Cretaceous
Diet: fish, squid
Habitat: open ocean
Fossil finds: North America (Alberta, Canada), Greenland, Europe (England, Germany), South America

IGUANODON "IGUANA TOOTH"

Pronunciation: ig-WA-no-DON
Maximum length: 12 m (40 ft)
Time: Early Cretaceous
Diet: leaves, branches, fronds, ferns
Habitat: woodlands
Fossil finds: Europe, North Africa, Asia (Mongolia), North America

KRONOSAURUS "KRONO'S LIZARD"

Pronunciation: kro-no-SAW-rus
Maximum length: 9 m (30 ft)
Time: Early Cretaceous
Diet: marine reptiles, fish, molluscs
Habitat: open ocean
Fossil finds: Australia (Queensland), South America (Columbia)

LAMBEOSAURUS "LAMBE'S LIZARD"

Pronunciation: LAM-bee-oh-SAW-rus
Maximum length: 15 m (49 ft)
Time: Late Cretaceous
Diet: pine needles, leaves, twigs
Habitat: forests
Fossil finds: North America (Montana, USA; Alberta, Canada), Mexico (Baja California)

LEAELLYNASAURA "LEAELLYN'S LIZARD"

Pronunciation: lee-AL-in-ah-SAW-ra
Maximum length: 3 m (10 ft)
Time: Middle Cretaceous
Diet: plants
Habitat: cold, icy regions
Fossil finds: Australia (Victoria)

LESOTHOSAURUS "LESOTHO LIZARD"

Pronunciation: leh-SOTH-uh-SAW-rus
Maximum length: 1 m (3 ft)
Time: Early Jurassic
Diet: low-lying plants
Habitat: semi-deserts
Fossil finds: South America (Venezuela), southern Africa (Lesotho)

MAIASAURA "GOOD MOTHER LIZARD"

Pronunciation: MY-a-SAW-ra
Maximum length: 9 m (30 ft)
Time: Late Cretaceous
Diet: plants
Habitat: wooded riverbanks
Fossil finds: North America

MAMENCHISAURUS "MAMEXI LIZARD"

Pronunciation: ma-MENCH-ih-SAW-rus
Maximum length: 25 m (82 ft)
Time: Late Jurassic
Diet: plants
Habitat: flood plain
Fossil finds: Asia (China)

MEGALOSAURUS "GREAT LIZARD"

Pronunciation: MEG-a-low-SAW-rus
Maximum length: 9 m (30 ft)
Time: Middle Jurassic
Diet: meat
Habitat: coastal woodland
Fossil finds: Europe (UK, France), Africa (Morocco)

MUSSAURUS "MOUSE LIZARD"

Pronunciation: muss-AW-rus
Maximum length: 3 m (10 ft)
Time: Late Triassic
Diet: plants
Habitat: dry desert
Fossil finds: South America (Argentina)

NOTHOSAURUS "SOUTHERN LIZARD"

Pronunciation: NOTH-uh-SAW-rus
Maximum length: 3 m (10 ft)
Time: Triassic
Diet: fish
Habitat: shallow tropical seas
Fossil finds: Europe (Germany, Italy, The Netherlands, Switzerland), North Africa, Asia, (Russia, China, Israel)

ORODROMEUS "MOUNTAIN RUNNER"

Pronunciation: OR-ro-DRO-me-us
Maximum length: 2.5 m (8 ft)
Time: Late Cretaceous
Diet: plants
Habitat: open woodland
Fossil finds: North America (Montana)

OURANOSAURUS "BRAVE LIZARD"

Pronunciation: OO-RAN-oh-SAW-rus
Maximum length: 7 m (23 ft)
Time: Early Cretaceous
Diet: plants
Habitat: flood plains
Fossil finds: Africa (Niger)

OVIRAPTOR "EGG ROBBER"

Pronunciation: OVE-ih-RAP-tor
Maximum length: 2.5 m (8 ft)
Time: Late Cretaceous
Diet: meat, eggs
Habitat: semi-desert
Fossil finds: central Asia (Mongolia)

PACHYCEPHALOSAURUS "THICK-HEADED LIZARD"

Pronunciation: PAK-ee-KEF-al-oh-SAW-rus
Maximum length: 4.6 m (15 ft)
Time: Late Cretaceous
Diet: leaves, fruit, small animals
Habitat: forests
Fossil finds: North America (USA; Alberta, Canada), Europe (UK), Asia (Mongolia), Africa (Madagascar)

PACHYRHINOSAURUS "THICK-NOSED LIZARD"

Pronunciation: PAK-ee-RINE-oh-SAW-rus
Maximum length: 7 m (23 ft)
Time: Late Cretaceous
Diet: cycads and other plants
Habitat: forests
Fossil finds: North America (Alberta, Canada, and Alaska, USA)

PARASAUROPHOLUS "BESIDE SAUROPHOLUS"

Pronunciation: par-a-SAWR-oh-LOAF-us
Maximum length: 12 m (40 ft)
Time: Late Cretaceous
Diet: pine needles, leaves, twigs
Habitat: swamps
Fossil finds: North America (New Mexico and Utah, USA; Alberta, Canada)

PENTACERATOPS "FIVE-HORNED FACE"

Pronunciation: PEN-ta-SER-a-tops
Maximum length: 8 m (26 ft)
Time: Late Cretaceous
Diet: cycads, palms, and other plants
Habitat: swamps, forests
Fossil finds: North America (New Mexico)

PHUWIANGOSAURUS "PHU WIANG LIZARD"

Pronunciation: poo-WYAHNG-o-SAW-rus
Maximum length: 30 m (102 ft)
Time: Early Cretaceous
Diet: plants
Habitat: tropical woodland
Fossil finds: Asia (Thailand)

PLATEOSAURUS "FLAT LIZARD"

Pronunciation: PLAT-ee-oh-SAW-rus
Maximum length: 8 m (26 ft)
Time: Late Triassic
Diet: conifers, cycads, and other plants
Habitat: dry desert

PROTOCERATOPS "FIRST-HORNED FACE"

Pronunciation: pro-toe-SER-a-tops
Maximum length: 2.5 m (8 ft)
Time: Late Cretaceous
Diet: plants
Habitat: desert-like scrubland
Fossil finds: Asia (Mongolia, China)

PSITTACOSAURUS "PARROT LIZARD"

Pronunciation: si-TAK-oh-SAW-rus
Maximum length: 2.5 m (8 ft)
Time: Early Cretaceous
Diet: plants, small animals
Habitat: desert-like scrubland
Fossil finds: Asia (Mongolia, China, Thailand)

PTERANODON "WINGED AND TOOTHLESS"

Pronunciation: ter-AN-uh-don
Wingspan: 9 m (30 ft)
Time: Late Cretaceous
Diet: fish, molluscs, shore animals
Habitat: shallow intercontinental seas
Fossil finds: North America (South Dakota, Kansas, Oregon in USA), Europe (England), Asia (Japan)

PTERODACTYLUS "WINGED FINGER"

Pronunciation: TER-uh-DAK-ti-lus
Wingspan: 1 m (3 ft)
Time: Late Jurassic
Diet: fish, insects
Habitat: coastal plains and cliffs
Fossil finds: Europe (England, France, Germany), Africa (Tanzania)

RHAMPHORHYNCHUS "BEAK SNOUT"

Pronunciation: RAM-for-RINE-cus
Wingspan: 1.75 cm (4 in)
Time: Late Jurassic
Diet: fish
Habitat: coastal plains and cliffs
Fossil finds: Europe (Germany, England), Africa (Tanzania)

SALTASAURUS "SALTA PROVINCE LIZARD"

Pronunciation: SALT-a-SAW-rus
Maximum length: 12 m (40 ft)
Time: Late Cretaceous
Diet: plants
Habitat: lowlands
Fossil finds: South America (Argentina, Uruguay)

SCELIDOSAURUS "LIMB LIZARD"

Pronunciation: skel-IDE-oh-SAW-rus
Maximum length: 4 m (13 ft)
Time: Early Jurassic
Diet: plants
Habitat: river valleys
Fossil finds: Europe, North America (Arizona, USA)

SEISMOSAURUS "QUAKE LIZARD"

Pronunciation: SIZE-mo-SAW-rus
Maximum length: 52 m (171 ft)
Time: Late Jurassic
Diet: conifers and other plants
Habitat: flood plain

SPINOSAURUS "SPINY LIZARD"

Pronunciation: SPINE-O-SAW-rus
Maximum length: 15 m (49 ft)
Time: Middle Cretaceous
Diet: fish, other dinosaurs, may have scavenged
Habitat: wooded river valleys
Fossil finds: Africa (Egypt, Morocco)

STEGOSAURUS "ROOF LIZARD"

Pronunciation: STEG-O-SAW-rus
Maximum length: 9 m (30 ft)
Time: Late Jurassic
Diet: low-lying plants
Habitat: open woodland
Fossil finds: North America (Utah, Wyoming, Colorado), Europe (UK), Asia (India, China), Africa

STYRACOSAURUS "SPIKED LIZARD"

Pronunciation: sty-RAK-oh-SAW-rus
Maximum length: 5 m (16 ft)
Time: Late Cretaceous
Diet: ferns, cycads, and other plants
Habitat: open woodland
Fossil finds: North America (Arizona and Montana, USA; Alberta, Canada)

SUCHOMIMUS "CROCODILE MIMIC"

Pronunciation: SOOK-O-MIEM-us
Maximum length: 11 m (36 ft)
Time: Early Cretaceous
Diet: fish, meat
Habitat: flood plain
Fossil finds: Africa (Niger)

THESCELOSAURUS "WONDERFUL LIZARD"

Pronunciation: THES-kel-O-SAW-rus
Maximum length: 4 m (13 ft)
Time: Late Cretaceous
Diet: plants
Habitat: wooded lowlands
Fossil finds: North America (Montana, South Dakota, and Wyoming, USA; Alberta and Saskatchewan, Canada)

TITANOSAURUS "TITAN LIZARD"

Pronunciation: tie-TAN-oh-SAW-rus
Maximum length: 20 m (66 ft)
Time: Late Cretaceous
Diet: plants
Habitat: open plains
Fossil finds: South America (Argentina), Europe (France), Asia (India), Africa (Madagascar)

TRICERATOPS "HORRIBLE THREE-HORNED FACE"

Pronunciation: try-SER-a-tops
Maximum length: 9 m (30 ft)
Time: Late Cretaceous
Diet: low-lying plants
Habitat: forests
Fossil finds: western North America

TROODON "WOUNDING TOOTH"

Pronunciation: TROE-o-don
Maximum length: 3.5 m (11 ft)
Time: Late Cretaceous
Diet: meat
Habitat: open woodland
Fossil finds: North America (Montana and Wyoming, USA; Alberta, Canada)

TROPEOGNATHUS "KEEL JAW"

Pronunciation: TRO-peog-NA-thus
Wingspan: 6 m (20 ft)
Time: Early Cretaceous
Diet: fish, squid
Habitat: open ocean
Fossil finds: South America (Brazil)

TYLOSAURUS "SWOLLEN LIZARD"

Pronunciation: TIE-lo-SAW-rus
Wingspan: 8 m (26 ft)
Time: Late Cretaceous
Diet: fish, squid, turtles
Habitat: open ocean
Fossil finds: North America (Manitoba, Northwest Territories, Kansas, Colorado, Alabama, Mississippi), Europe (Belgium)

TYRANNOSAURUS "TYRANT LIZARD"

Pronunciation: tie-RAN-oh-SAW-rus
Maximum length: 12 m (39 ft)
Time: Late Cretaceous
Diet: hunted and scavenged meat
Habitat: forests
Fossil finds: western North America, Asia (Mongolia)

VELOCIRAPTOR "SPEEDY THIEF"

Pronunciation: vel-O-si-RAP-tor
Maximum length: 2 m (6 ft)
Time: Late Cretaceous
Diet: meat, including other dinosaurs
Habitat: dry desert
Fossil finds: Asia (Mongolia, China)

VULCANODON "VULCAN TOOTH"

Pronunciation: vul-KAN-oh-don
Maximum length: 6.5 m (21 ft)
Time: Early Jurassic
Diet: plants
Habitat: dry savannah
Fossil finds: Africa (Zimbabwe)

XUANHANOSAURUS "XUANHAN COUNTY LIZARD"

Pronunciation: zwan-HAN-o-SAW-rus
Maximum length: 6 m (20 ft)
Time: Middle Jurassic
Diet: meat
Habitat: wet lowland areas
Fossil finds: Asia (China)

profiles

BIOGRAPHIES

Palaeontology is the science of extinct forms of life. In order to find out about extinct animals and plants, a palaeontologist has to be a naturalist, geologist, historian, archaeologist, zoologist, biologist – or a combination of some or all of these. On these pages, you will find the biographies of some of the palaeontologists and other scientists who have contributed to our extensive knowledge of the extraordinary world of the dinosaurs.

biographies

GEORGES LOUIS LECLERC, COMTE DE BUFFON
1707–1788

This French naturalist and author popularized natural history. His treatise *Histoire Naturelle* (*Natural History*) has appeared in several editions and has been translated into many languages. He was able to express complex ideas in a clear form, and his enthusiasm for the Jardin du Roi while he was keeper was so great that he made the gardens the centre of botanical research in France.

GEORGES CUVIER
1769–1832

The founder of comparative anatomy, French naturalist Baron Georges Cuvier led the way in the reconstruction of vertebrate animals. He systematically classified molluscs, fish, and fossil mammals and reptiles. He wrote on the structure of living and fossil animals, and believed that the development of life on Earth was greatly affected by occasional catastrophes. With Alexandre Brongniart, he explored the geology of the Paris Basin.

ALEXANDRE BRONGNIART
1770–1847

A French mineralogist, geologist, and chemist, Brongniart was the first to develop a systematic study of trilobites and a system for the classification of reptiles. Working with Georges Cuvier, he pioneered stratigraphy, the examination of rock layers to reveal past environments and life forms. In 1822, Brongniart and Cuvier mapped the Tertiary strata of the Paris Basin and collected local fossils.

WILLIAM BUCKLAND
1784–1856

This English clergyman and geologist dedicated himself to a systematic examination of the geology of Great Britain. In 1819, he discovered the first *Megalosaurus*, although he did not recognize it as a dinosaur. He wrote extensively about his finds and his treatise *Geology and Mineralogy* (1836) went through three editions. In 1845, he was appointed Dean of Westminster Abbey.

GIDEON MANTELL
1790–1852

A very successful doctor on the south coast of England, Mantell was also an amateur fossil hunter, one of the first in the world. His wife, Mary Ann Mantell, is thought to have found the first *Iguanodon* tooth in 1822, but it took many years for Mantell to establish its identity. He also discovered the first brachiosaur, *Pelorosaurus*, and *Hylaeosaurus*, an early ankylosaur.

MARY ANNING
1799–1847

A pioneering fossil collector, Anning's father sold fossil specimens in Lyme Regis on the south coast of England. It was there that she discovered the first *Ichthyosaurus* in 1811, and went on to discover the first plesiosaur in 1821 and the first pterodactyl in 1828.

RICHARD OWEN
1804–1892

Trained as a doctor, Owen went on to become an expert in comparative anatomy. He worked for the British Museum and founded the Natural History Museum in London. A pioneer in vertebrate palaeontology, he conducted extensive research on extinct reptiles, mammals, and birds. He coined the word "dinosaur" in 1842, and was responsible for the first full-scale dinosaur reconstructions, which were displayed in Crystal Palace Gardens in London.

DOUGLAS AGASSIZ
1807–1873

In 1826, Agassiz, a Swiss-American naturalist, was chosen to classify a large collection of fish that had been captured in the Amazon River region of Brazil, South America. He then researched in detail the extinct fish of Europe. By 1844, he was established as a pioneer in the study of extinct life, and had named nearly 1,000 fossil fish.

CHARLES DARWIN
1809–1882

English naturalist Charles Darwin's ideas are now the cornerstone of palaeontological research worldwide. In 1831, he travelled to the Galapagos Islands aboard the HMS *Beagle*, as a naturalist for a surveying expedition. His observations on the relationship between living animals, newly extinct animals, and fossil finds led him to develop a theory of evolution, a theory that was very controversial at the time. He believed that species evolve by a process of natural selection. His theories were published in 1859, in *On the Origin of Species by Natural Selection*, and *The Descent of Man* followed in 1871.

CHARLES OTHNIEL MARSH
1831–1899

After studying geology and palaeontology in Germany, this American palaeontologist was appointed professor of palaeontology at Yale University in 1860. He persuaded his uncle, George Peabody, to establish the Peabody Museum of Natural History at Yale, and organized scientific expeditions to the western states of the USA. He and his great rival, Edward Drinker Cope, dominated fossil-hunting in the late 1880s. He named about 500 species of fossil animals. His finds include *Pterodactylus*, *Apatosaurus*, *Allosaurus*, and early horses.

ERNST HAECKEL
1834–1919

Biologist Ernst Haeckel was the first prominent German to support Darwin's theories of evolution. He also drew up a genealogical tree, laying out the relationship between the various orders of animals. He coined the word "phylum" for the major group to which all related classes of organisms belong. He traced the descent of humans from single-celled organisms through chimpanzees and so-called *Pithecanthropus erectus*, which he saw as the link between apes and human beings.

WILLIAM PARKER FOULKE   d.1865

This US scientist and dinosaur artist found the first US hadrosaur skeleton. The bones were found by workmen in New Jersey in 1838. Foulke heard of the discovery in 1858 and recognized its importance. Joseph Leidy named the dinosaur after him, as *Hadrosaurus foulkii*.

EDWARD DRINKER COPE   1840–1897

After teaching comparative zoology and botany in Pennsylvania from 1864 to 1867, Cope spent 22 years exploring the area between Texas and Wyoming, where he discovered several extinct species of fish, reptiles, and mammals. He worked for the US Geological Survey as a palaeontologist, studying the evolutionary history of the horse and of mammal teeth. He published more than 1,200 books and papers, and was the author of Cope's Law, which stated that over time species tend to become larger. He is also remembered for his famous rivalry with Charles Othniel Marsh. His finds include *Camarasaurus* and *Ceolophysis*.

LOUIS DOLLO   1857–1931

This Belgian civil engineer and palaeontologist was responsible for the first reconstruction of *Iguanodon*. In 1878, he worked alongside Louis De Pauw to study the *Iguanodon* skeletons found in a coalmine at the village of Bernissart in Belgium. He identified the thumb spike, which had originally been thought to be a horn. Dollo's law states that organisms can evolve specializations, but that these are later lost. For example, horses cannot re-evolve the side toes that they have lost.

EUGENE DUBOIS   1858–1940

A Dutch anatomist and geologist, Dubois was interested in human evolution and in 1887, travelled to the East Indies to look for ancient human remains. In 1891, he discovered the remains of Java Man, the first known fossils of the early human *Homo erectus*. He found a one-million-year-old jaw fragment, skullcap, and thigh bone of a hominid that had distinctive brow ridges and a flat, receding forehead. He named it *Pithecanthropus* ("apeman") *erectus*.

EBERHARD FRAAS   1862–1915

In 1900, when German naturalist Fraas was travelling through Tanzania (then called Tanganyika) he visited Tendaguru Hills and helped to excavate more than 250 tonnes of dinosaur bones. He also found *Efraasia*, a primitive plant-eating dinosaur named after him, in what is now Germany, and named *Procompsognathus* in 1915. With Charles Andrews he suggested that creodonts (primitive carnivores) were the ancestors of whales.

ERNST STROMER VON REICHENBACH   1870–1952

German palaeontologist Stromer discovered the first dinosaurs in Egypt between 1911 and 1914, in the Bahariya Oasis, southwest of Cairo. The original specimens of the spinosaurids that he found were destroyed in the Bayerische Staatssammnung Museum when Madrid was bombed in 1944. He later identified the giant meat-eater.

BARNUM BROWN   1873–1963

This US palaeontologist was one of the greatest dinosaur hunters of the 20th century. His finds include *Ankylosaurus*, *Anchiceratops*, *Corythosaurus*, *Saurolophus*, and the first *Tyrannosaurus* ever discovered. From 1910 to 1915, Brown recovered a spectacular variety of complete dinosaur skeletons from the Red Deer River in Alberta, Canada. In the 1930s, he excavated a wealth of Jurassic fossils at Howe Ranch, Wyoming. As assistant curator, Brown also acquired fossils from all over the world for the American Museum of Natural History. He worked not only throughout the United States, but in Canada, India, South America, and Ethiopia.

WILLIAM BEEBE   1877–1962

US biologist, explorer, author, and inventor. An enthusiastic fossil collector from childhood, Beebe was an explorer and naturalist who became curator of ornithology at New York Zoological Gardens in 1899. In 1915, he described a hypothetical ancestor to *Archaeopteryx*, which he called *Tetrapteryx*. He also proposed that the ornithomimosaur (bird mimic) dinosaurs, such as *Deinocheirus*, ate insects.

ROY CHAPMAN ANDREWS   1884–1960

US naturalist Andrews graduated in 1906 and then went to Alaska and Japan on expeditions for the American Museum of Natural History (AMNH). Between 1922 and 1925, he led four expeditions to the Gobi Desert in Outer Mongolia, where he pioneered the use of a new vehicle, the car, backed up by camel trains, to explore remote regions. His teams discovered the first-known fossilized dinosaur nests and hatchlings as well as the world's first *Velociraptor* skeleton. He became the director of the AMNH in 1934. His other finds include *Protoceratops*, *Oviraptor*, and *Saurornithoides*.

LOUIS LEAKEY   1903–1972
MARY LEAKEY   1913–1996

Husband and wife team Louis and Mary proved with their fossil finds that human evolution was centred on Africa. These British anthropologists also proved that the human species was older than had been thought. They were working in the Olduvai Gorge, Tanzania, in 1959, when Mary discovered a 1.7-million-year-old fossil hominid. Between 1960 and 1973, the Leakeys discovered remains of *Homo habilis*, which Louis theorized was a direct ancestor of modern humans. After their deaths, their son Richard Leakey (b.1944) continued their work. Finds include *Proconsul*, *Australopithecus boisei*, and *Homo habilis*.

MARTIN GLAESSNER   1906–1989

Glaessner was an Australian geologist who produced the first detailed descriptions of the Precambrian Ediacaran fossils from the Flinders Range mountains of southern Australia. In 1961, he recognized that the Ediacaran fossils were the oldest-known multicelled organisms.

LUIS ALVAREZ   1911–1988
WALTER ALVAREZ   b.1940

This US father (geologist) and son (physicist) team publicized the discovery of a worldwide layer of clay rich in the rare element iridium. This element was present in rocks from the K-T boundary, the border between the Cretaceous and Tertiary periods. They argued that the iridium was deposited when a meteorite hit the Earth. They speculated that this event may have been the reason the dinosaurs became extinct.

ELSO BARGHOORN b.1915

In 1956, this US palaeontologist discovered two-billion-year-old Precambrian gunflint fossils in Ontario. These are some of the best-preserved microfossils in the world and Barghoorn found them in silica-rich flint rocks. In 1968, he showed how fossils of biomolecules such as amino acids can be preserved in rocks.

ZOFIA KIELAN-JAWOROWSKA b.1925

A Polish palaeontologist, Kielan-Jaworowska was the first woman to organize and lead fossil-hunting expeditions to the Gobi Desert, which took place from 1963 to 1971. In Mongolia, she discovered sauropods, tarbosaurs, duckbilled dinosaurs, ostrich mimics, and rare mammals from the Cretaceous and early Tertiary. Her book *Hunting for Dinosaurs* (1969) has done much to popularize palaeontology worldwide, but particularly in Mongolia. Her finds include a *Protoceratops* fighting a juvenile *Velociraptor*.

JOSÉ F. BONAPARTE b.1928

This Argentinian palaeontologist has found and named many South American dinosaurs, including *Mussaurus* and *Saltasaurus*. In 1993, with Rodolfo Coria, he named *Argentinosaurus*.

RODOLFO CORIA (unknown)

Coria, an Argentinian palaeontologist, worked with José F. Bonaparte in Argentina, naming *Argentinosaurus*. He then went on to identify a giant predator, *Gigantosaurus*, whose remains were spotted in 1994 in the foothills of the Andes by an amateur fossil-hunter.

RINCHEN BARSBOLD b.1935

As Director of the Institute of Geology at the Mongolian Academy of Sciences, this Mongolian palaeontologist discovered many new dinosaurs. *Barsboldia*, a 10 m- (30 ft-) long duck-billed dinosaur which lived in Mongolia in the Late Cretaceous, was named after him in 1981. His other finds include *Conchoraptor*, *Anserimimus*, and *Gallimimus*.

DONG ZHI-MING b.1937

Dong, a Chinese palaeontologist, studied under the father of Chinese palaeontology, Yang Zhongdian. A prolific dinosaur fossil-hunter, Dong has led expeditions to the Gobi Desert and China's Yunnan province. His finds include *Yangchuanosaurus*, *Chungkingosaurus*, and *Archaeoceratops*.

PETER GALTON b.1942

English palaeontologist Galton successfully demonstrated that hadrosaurs such as *Maiasaura* and *Hadrosaurus* did not drag their tails, but used them to act as a counterbalance to their heads. In the 1970s, he suggested that birds and dinosaurs should be grouped together as the Dinosauria. His other finds include *Lesothosaurus* and *Aliwalia*.

ROBERT T. BAKKER b.1945

This charismatic US palaeontologist and film consultant has promoted a number of controversial and revolutionary theories, including that dinosaurs are the hot-blooded relatives of birds, rather than cold-blooded giant lizards. His reconstructions of dinosaurs show them standing upright, not dragging their tails. He has organized digs in many countries, including Colorado, Utah, and Montana in the USA, South Africa, Mongolia, Zimbabwe, and Canada. He has found the only complete *Apatosaurus* skull and a baby allosaur tooth in an *Apatosaurus* bone. As part of his mission to popularize dinosaurs, Bakker acted as consultant on Steven Spielberg's film *Jurassic Park*. His other finds include a baby *Tyrannosaurus* and a *Stegosaurus*.

JENNIFER CLACK b.1947

Clack examined Devonian fossils and showed that legs that evolved for navigating in water, later became adapted for walking on land. This English palaeontologist's finding revolutionized theories about tetrapods, the first vertebrate animals that had legs. She also discovered *Acanthostega* and *Eucritta*.

SUE HENDRICKSON b.1949

In South Dakota in 1990, US marine archaeologist and fossil-hunter Hendrickson found the largest and most complete *Tyrannosaurus* to date. The fossil is now displayed at the Chicago Field Museum and is known as "Sue".

PHILIP J. CURRIE b.1949

A Canadian palaeontologist, Currie is a curator at the Royal Tyrrell Museum of Palaeontology, Drumheller in Canada, and a major research scientist. He has written a number of dinosaur books including *Newest and Coolest Dinosaurs* (1998). He specializes in Permian fossil reptiles including diapsid reptiles from Africa and Madagascar, and early kinds of synapsids from Europe and the USA. Finds include *Caudipteryx*.

DEREK BRIGGS b.1950

Known for his work on the Middle Cambrian Burgess Shale, English palaeontologist Briggs described a number of arthropods found there. The Burgess Shale is a 530-million-year-old mudstone deposit in British Columbia. He has discovered, with others, several Burgess Shale sites, showing that the animals found there were common inhabitants of the Cumbrian seas.

ERIC BUFFETAUT b.1950

This French geologist worked on developing a complete picture of dinosaur evolution in Thailand. He discovered the oldest known sauropod dinosaur, *Isanosaurus attavipachi* from the Upper Triassic, and numerous dinosaur fossil footprints. In Europe, he found a giant pterosaur with a wingspan of 9 m (19.5 ft). He also found the first late Cretaceous birds in France.

PAUL SERENO b.1957

Sereno, a US palaeontologist, has discovered dinosaurs on five continents. He named the oldest-known dinosaur, *Eoraptor*, and found the first complete skull of *Herrerasaurus* in the foothills of the Andes in Argentina. His team also found *Afrovenator* and the gigantic skull of *Carcharodontosaurus* in the Sahara. He has also been on expeditions to the Gobi Desert and India. He has rearranged the dinosaur family tree, reorganizing the ornithischians and naming the clade Cerapoda.

LUIS CHIAPPE b.1962

Argentinian vertebrate palaeontologist, and curator of vertebrate palaeontology at the Los Angeles County Museum, Chiappe is one of the world's leading authorities on ancient birds, and on the relationship between birds and dinosaurs. In 1998, in the Rio Colorado region of Patagonia, Chiappe's team unearthed thousands of *Titanosaurus* eggshells and the first dinosaur embryos to be found in the southern hemisphere. They also found the first identified eggs belonging to sauropods.

biographies

GLOSSARY

Adaptation the response of a living organism to changes in its environment.

Age a unit of geological time, which is characterized by some feature (like an Ice Age).

Amber a yellowish, fossilized tree resin that sometimes contains trapped matter.

Ammonite an early marine creature. It was protected by a spiral-coiled shell, which contained many air-filled chambers.

Amphibians animals that live in the water during their early life (breathing through gills), but usually live on land as adults (and breathe with lungs), for example frogs and salamanders.

Bipeds animals that walk on two legs are bipeds. Many carnivorous dinosaurs were bipedal, including *T. rex*.

Body fossils fossilized body parts, such as bones, teeth, claws, skin, and embryos.

Carnivores carnivores are animals that eat meat. They usually have sharp teeth and powerful jaws. All the theropods were carnivores, and some were hunters, while others scavenged.

Cold-blooded animals that rely upon the temperature and their behaviour (like sunning themselves) to regulate their body temperature are cold-blooded.

Coprolite ("dung stone") fossilized faeces. Coprolites record the diet and habitat of prehistoric animals.

Cretaceous Period the last period in the Mesozoic Era, from 145 to 65 million years ago. Flowering plants flourished and dinosaurs were at their height during the Cretaceous Period. There was a mass extinction at the end of the Cretaceous, marking the end of the dinosaurs and many other species of animals and plants.

Cycads primitive seed plants that dominated the Jurassic landscape. They have palm-like leaves and produce large cones.

Dinosaurs ("terrible lizard") extinct land reptiles that walked with an erect stance during the Mesozoic Era. Their hip structure caused their legs to stick out from under their bodies, and not sprawl out from the side like other reptiles.

Encephalization Quotient (EQ) the ratio of the brain weight of the animal to the brain weight of a similar animal of the same body weight.

Evolution a process in which the gene pool of a population gradually (over millions of years) changes in response to environmental pressures, natural selection, and genetic mutations. All forms of life came into being by this process.

Extinction the process in which groups of organisms (species) die out. Species go extinct when they are unable to adapt to changes in the environment or compete effectively with other organisms.

Fossils mineralized impressions or casts of ancient plants and animals (or their traces, like footprints).

Gastroliths stones that some animals swallow and use to help grind up tough plant matter in their digestive system are called gastroliths. They are also called gizzard rocks.

Ginkgo a primitive seed-bearing tree that was common during the Mesozoic Era. A deciduous tree, it has fan-shaped leaves.

Gondwana the southern continent formed after Pangaea broke up during the Jurassic Period. It included what are now the continents South America, Africa, India, Australia, and Antarctica.

Herbivores Animals that eat plants. Most dinosaurs were herbivores.

Horsetail a primitive, spore-bearing plant that was common during the Mesozoic Era. Its side branches are arranged in rings along the hollow stem. Horsetails date from the Devonian Period 408-360 million years ago, but are still around today and are invasive weeds.

Index fossils index fossils are commonly found fossils that existed during a limited time span. They help in dating other fossils.

Iridium this is a heavy metal element that is rare on the Earth's surface, but abundant on meteors and in the Earth's core.

Jurassic Period the second period of the Mesozoic Era, from 200 to 145 million years ago. Birds and flowering plants evolved, and many dinosaurs flourished during the Jurassic Period.

K-T Boundary boundary between the Cretaceous and Tertiary periods, about 65 million years ago. This was a time of the huge mass extinction of the dinosaurs.

Laurasia this was the northern supercontinent formed after Pangaea broke up during the Jurassic Period. Laurasia included what are now North America, Europe, Asia, Greenland, and Iceland.

Mammals these are hairy, warm-blooded animals that nourish their young with milk. Mammals evolved during the Triassic Period. People are mammals.

Mesozoic Era this is a major geological time span, from 250 to 65 million years ago. It is informally known as the Age of the Dinosaurs. The Mesozoic is sub-divided into the Triassic, Jurassic, and Cretaceous periods.

Ornithischians ("bird-hipped") dinosaurs that had a hip structure similar to that of birds. The two lower bones on each side lie parallel and point backwards. They were also herbivores.

Ornithopods mainly bipedal ornithischian dinosaurs that developed special teeth to grind up tough plant food.

Palaeontologist a scientist who studies the forms of life that existed in former geological periods, mainly by studying fossils.

Pangaea a supercontinent consisting of all of Earth's landmasses. It existed during the Permian Period through the Jurassic Period. It began breaking up during the Jurassic, forming the continents Gondwana and Laurasia.

Prosauropods plant-eating saurischians with long necks and thumb claws.

Quadruped animals that walk on four legs are quadrupeds. Most of the horned, armoured, and plated dinosaurs were quadrupeds.

Reptile a group of animals that have scales, breathe air, and, usually, lay eggs.

Saurischians ("lizard-hipped") the ancestors of birds, these dinosaurs had a hip structure similar to that of lizards – the two lower bones on each side point in opposite directions.

Sauropods large, quadrupedal plant-eating saurischians. They had long necks and tails.

Scavenger animals that eat dead animals that they did not kill themselves. Hyenas are modern-day scavengers.

Stratigraphy a method of dating fossils by observing how deeply a fossil is buried. Generally, deeper rocks and fossils are older than those found above them.

Theropods a group of saurischian dinosaurs that includes all the carnivores. Almost all the theropods were bipedal.

Trackways a series of footprints left behind as an animal walks over soft ground. They can indicate the animal's speed, weight, and herding behaviour.

Triassic Period the first period in the Mesozoic Era, from 250 to 200 million years ago. Dinosaurs and mammals evolved during the Triassic Period.

INDEX

ACKNOWLEDGEMENTS

Dorling Kindersley would like to thank Selina Wood for editorial assistance; Alyson Lacewing for proof-reading; Ann Barrett for the index; Jenny Siklos for Americanization; and Tony Cutting for DTP support.

Picture Credits

The publisher would like to thank the following for their kind permission to reproduce their photographs:

Abbreviations key:

t-top, b-bottom, r-right, l-left, c-centre, a-above, f-far

1 DK Images: Jonathan Hateley. **7** DK Images: Royal Tyrell Museum, Canada br. **8-9** DK Images: Jonathan Hateley. **9** DK Images: Natural History Museum cr; State Museum of Nature cr. **10** Corbis: Macduff Everton bl. **11** Corbis: Paul Funston; Gallo Images br. The Natural History Museum, London: tr.

12 DK Images: Natural History Museum tr. **13** DK Images: Natural History Museum c, bc. **13** N.H.P.A.: Joe Blossom cr. **15** Corbis: Galen Rowell br; Scott T. Smith t. Natural History Museum Basel: tr, bl. **16-17** DK Images: Bedrock Studios bc; Frank Denota c. **17** DK Images: Bedrock Studios tl, b; Natural History Museum tr. **18** Corbis: Charles Mamzy cfl; Gordon Whitten cl. DK Images: Bedrock Studios bcl; Jon Hughes br; Peter Winfield tl, tr. Science Photo Library: Ron Watts cfr. **19** Corbis: cb; Brenda Tharp bcr; Darrell Gulin tr; tl. DK Images: Jon Hughes bl, bc; Peter Winfield cr; Royal Tyrell Museum, Canada bc. **20** Corbis: David Pu'u cb. Katz/FSP: Eisermann/Life cr. The Natural History Museum, London: cra. Science Photo Library: Soames Summerhays bl. **20-21** Kobal Collection: Dreamworks/Paramount c. **21** Science Photo Library: Catherine Pouedras/Eurelios cbr; Geological Survey, Canada cr; Prof Walter Alvarez br. **24** The Natural History Museum, London: cl, crb. Science Photo Library: cr; George Barnard bc. **24-25** Institut Royal des Sciences Naturalles de Belgique: background. **25** American Museum Of Natural History: br. DK Images: Senekenberg Nature Museum bl. Mary Evans Picture Library: cl. Institut Royal des Sciences Naturalles de Belgique: tr, cra, cr. **26** Corbis: David Muench tl; James L. Amos ca; Philippe Eranian bl; Reuters/Carlos Barria cb. **27** Corbis: Bettmann ca; Dutheil Didier tr. Science Photo Library: Peter Menzel cb, br. Knight Rider/Tribune Media Services: William Hammer bl. **28** Judith River Dinosaur Institute: Judith River Dinosaur Institute c, crb, b, t. **28-29** Judith River Dinosaur Institute: Judith River Dinosaur Institute. **29** Homer Montgomery, National Park Services, US Department of the Interior: Homer

Montgomery, National Park Services, US Department of the Interior r. Judith River Dinosaur Institute: Judith River Dinosaur Institute c, bl. **31** Judith River Dinosaur Institute: Judith River Dinosaur Institute tr. Science Photo Library: Paul Fisher/North Carolina Museum of Natural Sciences/SPL br. **32** DK Images: Dinosaur State Park cl. The Natural History Museum, London: cl. **33** Museum of the Rockies: tl, car. Science Photo Library: Nieves Lopez/Eurelios cbl. **34** Corbis: Tom Bean l. **36** The Field Museum: The Field Museum tl, tr, bl, br. **36-37** The Field Museum: The Field Museum **37** The Field Museum: The Field Museum t; The Field Museum, courtesy Chris Brochu c, b. **38-39** Corbis: David Muench b; Kevin Schafer t; Tom Bean c. **39** Earth Sciences, University of Cambridge: Dr. James Hobro/Cambridge Earth Sciences, courtesy of Dr. James Miller cl. Science Photo Library: Geoff Tompkinson br. **43** DK Images: Royal Tyrrell Museum, Canada br. **45** DK Images: Natural History Museum tl; Senekenberg Nature Museum cr. **50-51** Science Photo Library: Smithsonian Museum t. **51** Copyright Peabody Museum of Natural History Yale University All Rights Reserved t. **53** DK Images: Graham High and Centaur Studios tl. **55** The Natural History Museum, London: cl. **56** Corbis: Michael S. Yamashita bl. DK Images: Peabody Museum of Natural History Yale University bc; Photo: Colin Keates cr. N.H.P.A.: Jonathan & Angela Scott br. Oxford Scientific Films: Highlights For Children tr. **57** Corbis: George H. H. Huey tr. DK Images: Jon Hughes t. Science Photo Library: Simon Fraser ca, b. **58** Corbis: Frank Trapper bl. **58-59** Natural Visions: Richard Coombers background. **61** Oxford Scientific Films: Matthias Brieter bl. **63** Corbis: Craig Aurness

background. The Natural History Museum, London: br. Jean Paul Ferrero bc. **64** DK Images: Jerry Young crb. N.H.P.A.: Martin Wendler bl. **64-65** Ardea.com: Francois Gohier; **65** DK Images: Philip Dowell cra. **66** The Field Museum: tr. **68** Prof. Anusuya Chinsamy-Turan: tl, tc, c. **70-71** Nakasato Museum: Sato Kazuhisa/Nakasato Museum, Japan. **73** FLPA: tr. **74** The Field Museum: The Field Museum, Chicago tl, bl. **74-75** Corbis: Charles Mauzy. **75** Corbis: Jonathan Blair t; Yann Arthus-Bertrand b. **76** Ardea.com: Francois Gohier bl. **76-77** Corbis: Theo Allofs t background. Oxford Scientific Films: Mark Deeble & Victoria Stone c. **77** Corbis: Brian A. Vikander br. Science Photo Library: Larry Miller c. Getty Images: Roine Magnusson bl. **78** DK Images: Gary Kevin t; Ray Moller bl. **79** American Museum Of Natural History: tr, tl. DK Images: Peter Winfield bl; Senekenberg Nature Museum: Andy Crawford br. **80-81** © Luis Rey. **81** Corbis: t. **82** Corbis: Bill Varie bl. Science Photo Library: Philippe Plailly/Eurelios cl, clb. Smithsonian Institution: cla; National Museum of Natural History/Chip Clark tl. **82-83** Corbis: Paul A. Souders. **83** Corbis: Jonathan Blair b.

Jacket images

Front: Corbis: Dutheil Didier (cr), Richard T. Nowitz (cfl); Science Photo Library: Roger Harris (cl). **Spine:** Science Photo Library: David Parker. **Back:** Corbis: Ferdaus Shamim (cfl); Science Photo Library: Chris Butler (cr), John Foster (cfr).

All other images © Dorling Kindersley. For further information see: www.dkimages.com